STUDY WORKBOOK FOR ISBN 978-1933039374

Foreclosure Prevention Loss Mitigation Specialist Training

©2012

Library of Congress -in-Publication Data
October 2012

Foreclosure Prevention – Loss Mitigation Specialist Study Workbook for ISBN 978-1933039374

Printed in the United States of America

10 9 8 7 6 5 4 3 2 1

The enclosed material is designed for educational purposes only. Each State may have different certification and specific guidelines. Please refer to your State for additional and future information. The information contained herein is considered correct at the time of creation but laws and regulations are updated frequently and the reader assumes the responsibility for confirming current regulations and applicable data. The publisher and author make no warranty as to the success of the individuals using the training material contained herein. The publisher and author make no warranty as to any action taken by any individual completing this program. The reader is responsible for the appropriate use of the materials and information provided. This publication is designed to provide accurate and authoritative information concerning the subject matter. All material is sold with the understanding that neither the author nor the publisher guarantees the actions of any individual making use of the inclusions. Neither the author nor the publisher is rendering a legal opinion, accounting recommendation or other professional service. If legal advice or other expert assistance is desired, the services of a legal professional or other individual should be sought. The applicable federally released forms, disclosures and notices are generated from public domain. Copyright law does apply to all intellectual materials and all rights under said law are reserved b y the copyright owner.

Coursework is available at special quantity discounts to use as premiums and sales promotions within corporate or private training programs. To obtain information or inquire about availability please write to Director, PO Box 1, Hollidaysburg, PA 16648.

STUDY WORKBOOK FOR ISBN 978-1933039374

Foreclosure Prevention Loss Mitigation Specialist Training

Flashcard Set

The flashcard set is designed to assist you in testing you retention of the materials. You should complete the coursework and then use a file card to cover the second row that contains the answers to each question. Review the questions and then check your answers.

When you feel you are ready for enhanced testing, complete the self-test segments of the workbook. Completing the self-tests without reference to the written text is the best method of assessing your knowledge base. If you are unable to answer a particular question, you should review the applicable chapter in its entirety.

What is a second mortgage?

A mortgage on the property that has a lien position behind the first mortgage

What is equity?

The value of a homeowner's unencumbered interest in real estate
Equity is the difference between the homes fair market value and the unpaid balance of the mortgage and any outstanding liens
Equity increases as the mortgage is paid down or as the property enjoys appreciation

What is a Foreclosure?

The legal process by which a homeowner in default on a mortgage is deprived of interest in the property This usually involves a forced sale of the property at public auction with the proceeds of the sale being applied to the mortgage debt

What is an Amortization Schedule ?

An Amortization Schedule is a timetable for the gradual repayment of a mortgage loan An amortization schedule indicates the amount of each payment applied to interest and principal, and the remaining balance after each payment is made.

What is Negative Amortization?

A gradual increase in mortgage debt that happens when a monthly payment does not cover the entire principal and interest due The shortfall is added to the remaining balance to create "negative" amortization

What is an Underwriter?

An underwriter is a company or person undertaking the responsibility for issuing a mortgage. Underwriters analyze a homeowner's credit worthiness and set the loan amount.

What is a Lifetime Rate Cap?

In an ARM, it limits the amount that the interest rate can increase or decrease over the life of the loan.

What is a mortgage servicer?

A mortgage servicer organization that collects monthly mortgage principal and interest payments from homeowners and manages escrow accounts for paying taxes and homeowners' insurance premiums
The servicer often services mortgages that have been purchased by an investor in the secondary mortgage market

Each work out option will have specific
qualifications applicable to

- The homeowner
- The property
- The lender
- All of the above

In order to be a viable option, each workout
option will have specific qualifications that
the homeowner, the property, and the
lender must meet.

What happens when a homeowner
refinances the mortgage?

Refinancing is the act a new loan in order
to pay off the existing mortgage or to gain
access to the existing equity in the home.

What is a HUD 1?

The document with an itemized listing of closing costs payable at the closing or settlement meeting when buying property   The closing costs can include a commission, loan fees, and points, and sums set aside for escrow payments, taxes, and insurance. It is signed by both the buyer and the seller, who may be paying some of the closing costs. The statement form is published by HUD

Which item is typically not an element of a forbearance plan?

- The homeowner stops making or reduces the monthly payment
- The homeowner suffers a financial crises with a definitive end
- The lender gets the opportunity to receive the full principal and interest owed from the homeowner
- None of the above

A forbearance plan enables the homeowner who has suffered a temporary financial setback that has a definitive end to halt making monthly payments or reduce the monthly payment amount until the end of the financial hardship. This plan enables the lender to begin receive full principal and interest payments from the homeowner a the end of the financial hardship.

What is PITI ?

PITI stands for principal, interest, taxes and insurance that are the usual components of a monthly mortgage payment.

The options negotiated during the loss mitigation process will depend on the

- resources of the homeowner
- term and type of hardship
- ultimate disposition of the property
- all of the above

The options negotiated during the loss mitigation process will depend on the resources of the homeowner, term and type of hardship, and ultimate disposition of the property.

What is a Depreciation?

A decline in the value of a property as opposed to appreciation

Negotiation of the forbearance option should be customized around the

- Needs of the homeowner
- Ability of the homeowner to pay
- Ultimate disposition of the homeowner
- All of the above

Negotiation of the forbearance option should be customized around the resources of the homeowner, term and type of hardship and the ultimate disposition plans for the property.

What is the term for a forbearance?

The terms of the forbearance will depend on the situation of the borrower, type and term of hardship, and the ultimate end planned for the forbearance. The end planned may be a resumption of payments or another loss mitigation intervention.

What is the Note?

The note is the document giving evidence of mortgage indebtedness, including the amount and terms of repayment.

What is the repayment option following a forbearance?

- Forgiveness
- Payment resumption plus catch up payments
- Refinance or capitalization
- Any of the above

The homeowner may negotiate a payment forgiveness, a resumption of payment plus catch up payments, or a refinance or capitalization of the amount owed as a result of the forbearance.

What is Negative Amortization?

Negative amortization is the gradual increase in mortgage debt that happens when a monthly payment does not cover the entire principal and interest due The shortfall is added to the remaining balance to create "negative" amortization.

What are the three primary responsibilities of the loss mitigation specialist?

- qualifying the homeowner
- obtaining verifications
- planning the negotiation package for remittal to the lender or loss mitigation supervisor

What is Assessed Value?

Assessed value is the value of a property as determined by a public tax assessor for the purpose of taxation.

What types of property are normally subject to loss mitigation actions?

- Second Homes
- Vacation Property
- Primary Residence
- Investment Property

Most lenders require that a property be an owner occupied, primary residence in order to qualify for loss mitigation actions.

What is the LTV?

Loan-to-Value Ratio is the ratio of a mortgage loan amount to the property's appraised value or selling price, whichever is less For example, if a home is sold for $100,000 and the mortgage amount is $80,000 the LTV is 80%

Explain the concept behind the property condition requirement often included in a forbearance negotiation.

The theory behind the property condition requirements are that many homeowners will be unable or unwilling to resume regular payments on a property whose condition is greatly deteriorated or whose value is exponentially lower than the mortgage principal balance.

What forms are commonly included within a forbearance package remittal?

- Hardship Verification
- Occupancy Status Verification
- DTI Assessments
- Surplus Income Assessments
- Credit Report
- Title Search
- Property Inspection and/or Appraisal

What is Lis Pendens?

A lis pendens is a pending lawsuit; in real estate, the constructive notice filed in public records that a legal dispute exists over a piece of property.

What is a loan modification?

Loan modification is a process where the lender and homeowner agree on new mortgage terms that are acceptable to both parties.

What is a common element of a loan modification?

- Lower Interest Rate
- Increased Loan Term
- Lower Principal Balance
- All of the Above

A loan modification may include lowering the interest rate, increasing the loan term, and lowering the principal balance of the loan.

The changes inherent in a loan modification are

- Temporary reductions to help overcome a hardship
- Long term changes to help offset an overextension of credit
- Permanent changes to the loan
- Any of the Above

The loan modification will be a permanent change to the loan of the homeowner.

What is a characteristic of a loan that is often a higher candidate for loan modification?

- a higher than market average interest rate
- an equity position that enables the capitalization of costs associated with the default or modification process
- a shorter-term repayment plan
- all of the above

Certain loans contain characteristics such as a higher than market interest rate, an equity position that enables the capitalization of costs, or a shorter repayment term. These characteristics make them a higher candidate for loan modification.

What type of loan does a homeowner typically obtain in a loan modification?

- Interest Only
- Fixed Rate
- Government Guaranteed
- None of the Above

Lenders will typically negotiate a modification that enables the homeowner to obtain a fully amortized, fixed rate loan.

What modification will have the greatest effect on the homeowner in a loan modification?

- Amortization Term
- Interest Rate
- Amortization Method
- All of the Above

The lowering of an interest rate, extension of an amortization term, and method of amortization applied to the loan balance may all have a dramatic effect on the homeowners ability to resume making timely payments against the mortgage note.

When qualifying a homeowner for a loan modification, the homeowner must illustrate

- That the homeowner desires the loan modification
- That a modification will enable the homeowner to resume making payments
- That the homeowners income is sufficient to pay the current mortgage and other debt
- All of the Above

When qualifying a homeowner for a loan modification, the homeowner must illustrate that a modification will enable the homeowner to resume making payments

What is a lien?

A lien is a legal hold or claim from one person on the property of another   The lien placed by a first mortgage is special. It is called a first lien and takes precedence over others.

A short refinance is the term used for a refinance when the homeowner is behind on payments.

- True
- False

FALSE – A short refinance is a combination loss mitigation workout that enables the homeowner to refinance the mortgage note at a lower principal balance than currently exists on the note. The property must have had a decrease in value to be eligible for a short refinance.

What is the Acceleration Clause?

A acceleration clause is the section of a mortgage document that allows the lender to speed up the payment date in the event of default, making the entire principal amount due.

A traditional refinance is a common loss mitigation workout option for homeowners who are only a few payments behind.

- True
- False

FALSE - The traditional refinance option is typically employed with those homeowners who contact the loss mitigation department before a default situation exists.

What is the Housing Expense?

The housing expense is the percentage of gross monthly income that goes toward paying a Ratio mortgage or rent on a home.

A product matrix is a valuable asset when screening a homeowner profile for a potential refinance.

- True
- False

TRUE – A product matrix is a snapshot of the minimum requirements needed to place a loan in a particular approval tier or level. You can easily complete a preliminary screening of the homeowner criteria using the product matrix.

A short sale dictates that the homeowner

- Offer the property for sale to the general public
- Maintain the property
- Actively market the property for sale
- All of the above

A short sale approval dictates that the homeowner offer the property for sale to the general market. During the sale process, the property owner must maintain the property and do everything within their power to market the property and facilitate a sale.

A short sale is the same as a foreclosure.

- True
- False

FALSE – A short sale is often termed a pre-foreclosure sale.

What is Marketable Title?

A title that is clear of liens, encumbrances and other defects.

If the short sale process nets less money than the total value of the note, the homeowner must make up the difference owed to the bank out of their own pocket.

- True
- False

FALSE – The pre-foreclosure loss mitigation process enables the homeowner to relinquish the property and negotiate to remove any accountability for any sale shortfalls that may result from the sale of the property in the current market.

In a pre-foreclosure sale, the lender agrees to accept the proceeds of a sale set a current fair market value as indicated by comparables and appraisals for the market of the property.

- True
- False

TRUE - In a pre-foreclosure sale, the lender agrees to accept the proceeds of a sale set a current fair market value as indicated by comparables and appraisals for the market of the property.

What is a Home Inspection?

A home inspection is an inspection by a building professional that evaluates the structural and mechanical condition of a property.

The short sale offering should be considered

- Whenever a homeowner fails to meet lesser loss mitigation workout options
- Whenever the homeowner feels that they no longer wish to retain the property
- Whenever the lender does not refuses a forbearance request
- All of the above

The short sale option should be considered as a workout option whenever a homeowner fails to meet lesser loss mitigation workout options.

What is a foreclosure?

A foreclosure is the legal process by which a homeowner in default on a mortgage is deprived of interest in the property This usually involves a forced sale of the property at public auction with the proceeds of the sale being applied to the mortgage debt.

Name four potential, verifiable reasons that a homeowner may need to vacate a property

---

Job Transfer
Divorce
Reduced Income
Death of One Party

A short sale is a potential solution if the homeowner feels they wish to walk away from their mortgage even though they have the capability to make the monthly payments required under the note.

- True
- False

FALSE – A homeowner would not qualify for a short sale workout if they have simply chosen the surrender option and do not meet the qualifying criteria of need set forth by the lender.

A requirement of the short sale process is that the _____ must show a ____ ____ _____ effort to sell the property.

A requirement of the short sale process is that the <u>homeowner</u> must show a <u>good</u> <u>faith</u> effort to sell the property.

The lender will require that a short sale appraisal illustrate that the value of the property is substantially less than the amount of the outstanding mortgage against the property.

- True
- False

TRUE – The short sale approval and sales price basis will be dependent on the appraisal completed on the property.

A short sale property must be

- In good cosmetic condition
- In good structural condition
- Comparable with similar homes for sale within the same area and at the same price
- Any of the Above

Most lenders will require that the homeowner complete necessary cosmetic repairs to the property and may reject a short sale option of the property requires extensive or costly structural or other repair work to bring it up to market standards.

The short sale term will be negotiated based on what common elements?

---

market conditions

property condition

sales price

any other information deemed applicable

A deed in lieu of foreclosure is another term used for the short sale.

- True
- False

FALSE - A deed in lieu of foreclosure dictates that the homeowner executes a deed that relinquishes their interest in the property to the lender in exchange for a satisfaction of the mortgage. The lender then offers the property for sale in the general market.

The deed in lieu of foreclosure is risky for the lender because the condition of the property may be such that it cannot be offered for sale without costly repairs.

- True
- False

FALSE – The DIL dictates that the homeowner will surrender possession of the property promptly, provide the lender with a deed transferring any and all interest held by the homeowner, and leave the property in good, marketable condition.

What is the benefit to the lender in a cash for keys transaction.

A homeowner may negotiate the payment of a stipulated amount of cash from the lender in exchange for leaving the property in broom clean condition (as is standard for traditional property transfers) and for vacating the property in a timely manner.

What is Equity?

Equity is the value of a homeowner's unencumbered interest in real estate. Equity is the difference between the homes fair market value and the unpaid balance of the mortgage and any outstanding liens Equity increases as the mortgage is paid down or as the property enjoys appreciation.

What is an Appraised Value?

An appraised value is the opinion of a property's fair market value, based on an appraiser's inspection and analysis of the property.

The initial contact

- sets the tone for your relationship with the borrower
- is the most essential information-gathering period
- sets the workout option you will use for the borrower
- none of the above

The initial contact is the most essential information-gathering period.

What is Depreciation?

Depreciation is a decline in the value of a property as opposed to appreciation

What type of lien is created against a property when an owner uses it as collateral to borrower money?

- General Lien
- Voluntary Lien
- Involuntary Lien
- All of the Above

A voluntary lien is created against a property when an owner uses it as collateral to borrower money.

A general lien goes against an individual and does not impact real property.

- True
- False

A general lien may affect any real estate owned by the individual who is the subject of the lien.

When a property is sold by order of the court it is termed a

- Judgment Lien
- Foreclosure
- Escheat
- All of the Above

When a property is sold by order of the court is it termed a foreclosure.

What does it mean to execute?

To validate a document.

Liens may be imposed against

- Fixtures
- Improvements
- Real Property
- All of the Above

Liens may be imposed against fixtures, improvements, and real property.

A quitclaim deed

- contains no warranties
- contains no covenants
- does not promise the seller even holds interest in the property
- all of the above

A quitclaim deed contains no warranties, covenants, or even the promise that the individual signing the deed holds any interest in the property.

A cession deed is a form of

- General Warranty Deed
- Quitclaim Deed
- Guardians Deed
- None of the Above

A cession deed is a form of Quitclaim Deed.

A deed restriction may limit

- the action of a lender
- the action of the owner
- the action of an investor
- all of the above

A deed restriction may limit the actions of any party gaining ownership or other interest in a property.

What is a Judgment?

The order by a court as to money owed or other definitive decisions.

Skill Enhancement Self-Tests

Loss Mitigation Self Test #1

Name:
_____

Date:
_____

Score:
_____

Instructor:
_____

1.   You should work out the loss mitigation option that contains the

_____

_____

_____

_____

_____

2.   Why have ethics and disclosure laws been created?

    a.   To provide the lender with a series of practical directions
    b.   To protect the interest of the public
    c.   To make the obtainment of mortgage funds a fair practice
    d.   All of the above

3.   What is an Adjustable Rate Mortgage?

_____

_____

_____

_____

_____

4.   A loss mitigation specialist acts as a _____ to facilitate _____
        _____between a homeowner who is in or about to enter default status on a
        mortgage loan and the lender.

.5.   What is an Amortization Schedule?

_____

_____

_____

_____

_____

_____

6.   A verification of deposit is a form sent

        a.   To the closing or settlement agent to verify the funds to close
        b.   To the bank to verify the average bank account balance of the borrower
        c.   to the real estate agent to verify the earnest money deposit
        d.   none of the above

7.   What is the HUD-1?

_____

_____

_____

_____

_____

_____

8. When qualifying a homeowner for a loan modification, the homeowner must illustrate

    a. That the homeowner desires the loan modification
    b. That a modification will enable the homeowner to resume making payments
    c. That the homeowners income is sufficient to pay the current mortgage and other debt
    d. All of the Above

9. What is Assessed Value?

    _____

    _____

    _____

    _____

    _____

    _____

10. Your most valuable tool in planning a loss mitigation starategy strategy is

    a. customer service skills
    b. information
    c. qualification skills
    d. loan knowledge

Loss Mitigation Self Test #2

Name:

Date:

Score:

Instructor:

1.   What is a Second Mortgage?

_____

_____

_____

_____

_____

_____

2.   Which item is typically not an element of a forbearance plan?
   a.   The homeowner stops making or reduces the monthly payment
   b.   The homeowner suffers a financial crises with a definitive end
   c.   The lender gets the opportunity to receive the full principal and interest owed
            from the homeowner
   d.   None of the above

3.   What is Negative Amortization?

_____

_____

_____

_____

_____

_____

4.   Credit Reports are:

      a.   A great way to see how many things people buy
      b.   A way to get to know a borrower's likes and dislikes
      c.   An overview of a person's entire history of spending and payment
      d.   None of the above

5.   What forms are commonly included within a forbearance package remittal?

_____

_____

_____

_____

_____

_____

6.   The changes inherent in a loan modification are

      a.   Temporary reductions to help overcome a hardship
      b.   Long term changes to help offset an overextension of credit
      c.   Permanent changes to the loan
      d.   Any of the Above

7.   What does a debt ratio tell you about a file?

_____

_____

_____

_____

_____

_____

8. Credit reports are an overview of a person's entire history of spending and payment habits.

    a. True
    b. False

9. What is a First mortgage?

    _____

    _____

    _____

    _____

    _____

    _____

10. Credit bureau scores are based upon

    a. Every action taken by a borrower with regard to debt
    b. The data contained within the credit bureau
    c. All information contained within the loan application
    d. None of the above

Loss Mitigation Self Test #3

Name:

Date:

Score:

Instructor:

1.   What is a front-end ratio?

_____

_____

_____

_____

_____

_____

2.   What is a lien?

_____

_____

_____

_____

_____

_____

3.   A short refinance is the term used for a refinance when the homeowner is behind on payments.

    a.   True
    b.   False

4.   Which ratio is defined as the gross income divided by the new PITI mortgage
      payment and the minimum monthly payment from all other liabilities?

      _____

      _____

      _____

      _____

      _____

      _____

5.   A competent loss mitigation specialist must

      _____

      _____

      _____

      _____

      _____

      _____

6.   A credit bureau score will rank order potential borrowers based upon the number of
      good loans to bad loans.

      a.   True
      b.   False

7.   How many times do you factor each debt when calculating debt ratios?

      _____

      _____

      _____

      _____

      _____

      _____

8.   What is Equity?

_____

_____

_____

_____

_____

_____

9.   The options negotiated during the loss mitigation process will depend on the

    a.   resources of the homeowner
    b.   term and type of hardship
    c.   ultimate disposition of the property
    d.   all of the above

10.   You will calculate the debt ratio using

    a. Gross Income
    b. Net Income
    c. Additional Income
    d. None of the above

Loss Mitigation Self Test #4

Name: _____

Date: _____

Score: _____

Instructor: _____

1.   Whose income and credit history do you use when calculating debt-to-income ratio for married applicants?

_____

_____

_____

_____

_____

_____

2.   What is the term for a forbearance?

_____

_____

_____

_____

_____

_____

3.   Debt to Income is

    a.   The amount of debt a borrower carries
    b.   The amount of income a borrower brings home
    c.   The amount of income a borrower makes before taxes
    d.   None of the above

4.   What is a Convertible Mortgage?

_____

_____

_____

_____

_____

_____

5.   Negotiation of the forbearance option should be customized around the

        a.   Needs of the homeowner
        b.   Ability of the homeowner to pay
        c.   Ultimate disposition of the home
        d.   All of the above

6.   Gross income is:

_____

_____

_____

_____

_____

_____

7.   What is PITI ?

_____

_____

_____

_____

_____

_____

8.   Occupancy Status will effect

    a. Approval Levels
    b. Underwriting Schedule
    c. Appraised Value
    d. All of the above

9.   What is an Amortization Term?

_____

_____

_____

_____

_____

_____

10.   What types of property are normally subject to loss mitigation actions?

    a.   Second Homes
    b.   Vacation Property
    c.   Primary Residence
    d.   Investment Property

Loss Mitigation Self Test #5

Name:

Date:

Score:

Instructor:

1. Explain the formula for factoring a potential mortgage payment.

_____

_____

_____

_____

_____

_____

2. What are the three primary responsibilities of the loss mitigation specialist?

_____

_____

_____

_____

_____

3. URAR is an abbreviation for

    a. The Uniform Residential Appraisal Report
    b. The 1004
    c. The most common appraisal you will encounter
    d. All of the above

4.   What is an Appraised Value?

_____

_____

_____

_____

_____

_____

5.   What is a common element of a loan modification?

      a.   Lower Interest Rate
      b.   Increased Loan Term
      c.   Lower Principal Balance
      d.   All of the Above

6.   What is the repayment option following a forbearance?

_____

_____

_____

_____

_____

_____

7.   The appraiser will assess

      a. The property
      b. The neighborhood
      c. Recently sold property
      d. All of the above

8.   Why is an appraisal vital to the loss mitigation process?

_____

_____

_____

_____

_____

_____

9.   What is an Amortization Schedule?

_____

_____

_____

_____

_____

_____

10.   What is a characteristic of a loan that is often a higher candidate for loan
        modification?

        a.   a higher than market average interest rate
        b.   an equity position that enables the capitalization of costs associated with the
                default or modification process
        c.   a shorter-term repayment plan
        d.   all of the above

Loss Mitigation Self Test #6

Name:

Date:

Score:

Instructor:

1.   What is your goal when reviewing an appraisal?

_____

_____

_____

_____

_____

_____

2.   What is Negative Amortization?

_____

_____

_____

_____

_____

_____

3.   What is an Adjustment Interval?

_____

_____

_____

_____

_____

4. Property Valuation will be determined by

    a. Comparison with other property
    b. Sales price of other property
    c. Proximity to recently sold property
    d. All of the above

5. What is the Annual Percentage Rate (APR)?

_____

_____

_____

_____

_____

_____

6. What type of loan does a homeowner typically obtain in a loan modification?

    a. Interest Only
    b Fixed Rate
    c Government Guaranteed
    d None of the Above

7. What happens when a homeowner refinances the mortgage?

_____

_____

_____

_____

_____

_____

8.   A product matrix is

      a.   The final underwriting guideline manual
      b.   A snapshot of minimum requirements
      c.   A snapshot of final requirements
      d.   None of the above

9.   What is Depreciation?

_____

_____

_____

_____

_____

_____

10.   What modification will have the greatest effect on the homeowner in a loan modification?

      a.   Amortization Term
      b.   Interest Rate
      c.   Amortization Method
      d.   All of the Above

Loss Mitigation Self Test #7

Name:

Date:

Score:

Instructor:

1.   Each work out option will have specific qualifications applicable to

_____

_____

_____

_____

_____

_____

2.   What does the sales comparison valuation approach consider?

_____

_____

_____

_____

_____

_____

3.   A traditional refinance is a common loss mitigation workout option for homeowners who are only a few payments behind.

      a.   True
      b.   False

4.   What is the LTV?

_____

_____

_____

_____

_____

_____

5.   A product matrix is a valuable asset when screening a homeowner profile for a
      potential refinance.

      a.   True
      b.   False

6.   What is a Home Inspection?

_____

_____

_____

_____

_____

_____

7.   A short sale is a potential solution if the homeowner feels they wish to walk away
      from their mortgage even though they have the capability to make the monthly
      payments required under the note.

      a.   True
      b.   False

8. The short sale term will be negotiated based on what common elements?

_____

_____

_____

_____

_____

_____

9. The lender will require that a short sale appraisal illustrate that the value of the property is substantially less than the amount of the outstanding mortgage against the property.

    a.   True
    b.   False

10. What is an Appraised Value?

_____

_____

_____

_____

_____

_____

Loss Mitigation Self Test #8

Name: _____

Date: _____

Score: _____

Instructor: _____

1.   A deed in lieu of foreclosure is another term used for the short sale.

        a.   True
        b.   False

2.   What does it mean to execute?

_____

_____

_____

_____

_____

_____

3.   A short sale property must be

        a.   In good cosmetic condition
        b.   In good structural condition
        c.   Comparable with similar homes for sale within the same area and at the same
                price
        d.   Any of the Above

4.   What is a Judgment?

_____

_____

_____

_____

_____

_____

5.   A general lien goes against an individual and does not impact real property.

      a.   True
      b.   False

6.   What is Depreciation?

_____

_____

_____

_____

_____

_____

7.   Liens may be imposed against

      a.   Fixtures
      b.   Improvements
      c.   Real Property
      d.   All of the Above

8.   What is Equity?

_____

_____

_____

_____

_____

_____

9.   What type of lien is created against a property when an owner uses it as collateral to borrower money?

        a.   General Lien
        b.   Voluntary Lien
        c.   Involuntary Lien
        d.   All of the Above

10.   Name four potential, verifiable reasons that a homeowner may need to vacate a property

_____

_____

_____

_____

_____

_____

Loss Mitigation Self Test #9

Name:

Date:

Score:

Instructor:

1.   The initial contact

        a.   sets the tone for your relationship with the borrower
        b.   is the most essential information-gathering period
        c.   sets the workout option you will use for the borrower
        d.   none of the above

2.   What is a foreclosure?

_____

_____

_____

_____

_____

_____

3   A requirement of the short sale process is that the _____ must show a _____ effort to sell the property.

4.   What is Marketable Title?

_____

_____

_____

_____

_____

_____

5.   If the short sale process nets less money than the total value of the note, the homeowner must make up the difference owed to the bank out of their own pocket.

   a.   True
   b.   False

6.   What is the Housing Expense?

_____

_____

_____

_____

_____

_____

7.   Loss mitigation negotiations opens up the possibility of

_____

_____

_____

_____

_____

_____

8.   What is the Note?

_____

_____

_____

_____

_____

_____

9. A short sale dictates that the homeowner

    a. Offer the property for sale to the general public
    b. Maintain the property
    c. Actively market the property for sale
    d. All of the above

10. What is a loan modification?

    _____

    _____

    _____

    _____

    _____

    _____

Name:

Date:

Score:

Instructor:

1.   A short sale is the same as a foreclosure.

        a.   True
        b.   False

2.   What is the Acceleration Clause?

_____

_____

_____

_____

_____

_____

3.   In a pre-foreclosure sale, the lender agrees to accept the proceeds of a sale set a current fair market value as indicated by comparables and appraisals for the market of the property.

        a.   True
        b.   False

4.   What is Lis Pendens?

_____

_____

_____

_____

_____

_____

5.   The short sale offering should be considered

    a.   Whenever a homeowner fails to meet lesser loss mitigation workout options
    b.   Whenever the homeowner feels that they no longer wish to retain the property
    c.   Whenever the lender does not refuses a forbearance request
    d.   All of the above

6.   What is a mortgage servicer?

_____

_____

_____

_____

_____

_____

7.   The deed in lieu of foreclosure is risky for the lender because the condition of the property may be such that it cannot be offered for sale without costly repairs.

    a.   True
    b.   False

8.   What is the benefit to the lender in a cash for keys transaction.

_____

_____

_____

_____

_____

_____

9.   When a property is sold by order of the court it is termed a

        a.   Judgment Lien
        b.   Foreclosure
        c.   Escheat
        d.   All of the Above

10.   Explain the concept behind the property condition requirement often included in a forbearance negotiation.

_____

_____

_____

_____

_____

_____

Loss Mitigation Self Test #11

Name:

Date:

Score:

Instructor:

1.   A quitclaim deed

    a.   contains no warranties
    b.   contains no covenants
    c.   does not promise the seller even holds interest in the property
    d.   all of the above

2.   What is an Underwriter?

_____

_____

_____

_____

_____

_____

3.   A cession deed is a form of

    a.   General Warranty Deed
    b.   Quitclaim Deed
    c.   Guardians Deed
    d.   None of the Above

4.   What is a Forbearance Plan?

_____

_____

_____

_____

_____

_____

5.   A deed restriction may limit

      a.   the action of a lender
      b.   the action of the owner
      c.   the action of an investor
      d.   all of the above

6.   What is a Amortization Schedule ?

_____

_____

_____

_____

_____

_____

7.   The first step in the loss mitigation process is to

_____

_____

_____

_____

_____

_____

Self-Test Answer Keys

Loss Mitigation Answer Key #1

Name: _____

Date: _____

Score: _____

Instructor: _____

1. You should work out the loss mitigation option that contains the least intervention necessary to cure the default and stabilize the borrower.

2. D   All of the above

3. A mortgage in which the rate of interest is adjusted based on a standard rate index. Most ARM's have caps on how much the interest rate may increase

4. A loss mitigation specialist acts as a liaison to facilitate negotiations between a homeowner who is in or about to enter default status on a mortgage loan and the lender.

5. A timetable for the gradual repayment of a mortgage loan An amortization schedule indicates the amount of each payment applied to interest and principal, and the remaining balance after each payment is made

6. b.   To the bank to verify the average bank account balance of the borrower

7. The document with an itemized listing of closing costs payable at the closing or settlement meeting when buying property The closing costs can include a commission, loan fees, and points, and sums set aside for escrow payments, taxes, and insurance. It is signed by both the buyer and the seller, who may be paying some of the closing costs. The statement form is published by HUD

8. d.   All of the Above

9. Assessed value is the value of a property as determined by a public tax assessor for the purpose of taxation.

10. B   information

Loss Mitigation Answer Key #2

Name:

Date:

Score:

Instructor:

1.   A mortgage on the property that has a lien position behind the first mortgage

2.   d.   None of the above

3.   A gradual increase in mortgage debt that happens when a monthly payment does not cover the entire principal and interest due The shortfall is added to the remaining balance to create "negative" amortization

4.   C.   An overview of a person's entire history of spending and payment

5.   Hardship Verification
       Occupancy Status Verification
       DTI Assessments
       Surplus Income Assessments
       Credit Report
       Title Search
       Property Inspection and/or Appraisal

6.   The loan modification will be a permanent change to the loan of the homeowner

7.   How much loan borrowers can afford

8.   A True

9.   A mortgage that is the primary lien against a property

10.   B.   The data contained within the credit bureau

Name:

Date:

Score:

Instructor:

1.   The gross income divided by the new PITI mortgage payment

2.   A lien is a legal hold or claim from one person on the property of another   The lien placed by a first mortgage is special. It is called a first lien and takes precedence over others.

3.   FALSE – A short refinance is a combination loss mitigation workout that enables the homeowner to refinance the mortgage note at a lower principal balance than currently exists on the note. The property must have had a decrease in value to be eligible for a short refinance.

4.   The back end ratio

5.   A competent loss mitigation specialist must be able to assess the financial condition of the homeowner and the value of the property, gain an understanding of how each potential negotiation outcome will benefit and harm each party, and become adept at negotiating each level of the loss mitigation process.

6.   A.   True

7.   One time, regardless of the number of times the debt appears in the report(s).

8.   The value of a homeowner's unencumbered interest in real estate Equity is the difference between the homes fair market value and the unpaid balance of the mortgage and any outstanding liens Equity increases as the mortgage is paid down or as the property enjoys appreciation

9.   The options negotiated during the loss mitigation process will depend on the resources of the homeowner, term and type of hardship, and ultimate disposition of the property

10.   A. Gross Income

Loss Mitigation Answer Key #4

Name: _____

Date: _____

Score: _____

Instructor: _____

1.   Both parties' income and credit history is considered, but you factor each debt only once even if it appears on both credit reports.

2.   The terms of the forbearance will depend on the situation of the borrower, type and term of hardship, and the ultimate end planned for the forbearance. The end planned may be a resumption of payments or another loss mitigation intervention.

3.   D.   None of the above

4.   An adjustable rate mortgage ARM that can be converted to a fixed mortgage under specific conditions

5.   Negotiation of the forbearance option should be customized around the resources of the homeowner, term and type of hardship and the ultimate disposition plans for the property.

6.   Income before taxes

7.   PITI stands for principal, interest, taxes and insurance that are the usual components of a monthly mortgage payment.

8.   A. Approval Levels

9.   The amount of time required to amortize (repay) a mortgage loan. The amortization term is usually expressed in months. A 30-year fixed rate mortgage, for example, has an amortization term of 360 months

10.   Most lenders require that a property be an owner occupied, primary residence in order to qualify for loss mitigation actions.

Loss Mitigation Answer Key #5

Name: _____

Date: _____

Score: _____

Instructor: _____

1.   Gross monthly income x 29% (max qualifying ratio) = Max Mortgage Payment

2.   qualifying the homeowner
      obtaining verifications
      planning the negotiation package for remittal to the lender or loss mitigation
      supervisor

3.   a. The Uniform Residential Appraisal Report

4.   An opinion of a property's fair market value, based on an appraiser's inspection and
      analysis of the property

5.   A loan modification may include lowering the interest rate, increasing the loan term,
      and lowering the principal balance of the loan.

6.   The homeowner may negotiate a payment forgiveness, a resumption of payment plus
      catch up payments, or a refinance or capitalization
      of the amount owed as a result of the forbearance.

7.   D. All of the above

8.   Since the borrower has or is about to default on the loan, the property becomes the
      lenders primary means of recouping their funds.

9.   A timetable for the gradual repayment of a mortgage loan An amortization schedule
      indicates the amount of each payment applied to interest and principal, and the
      remaining balance after each payment is made

10.   Certain loans contain characteristics such as a higher than market interest rate, an
      equity position that enables the capitalization of costs, or a shorter repayment term.
      These characteristics make them a higher candidate for loan modification.

Name:

Date:

Score:

Instructor:

1.   To scrutinize any item that appears to vary between documents in the file and the entries on the appraisal to determine which document contains the error and to note any item that is below the minimum requirements of the loss mitigation guidelines.

2.   Negative amortization is the gradual increase in mortgage debt that happens when a monthly payment does not cover the entire principal and interest due The shortfall is added to the remaining balance to create "negative" amortization.

3.   How often the loan's rate can be changed

4.   D. All of the above

5.   A standardized method of calculating the cost of a mortgage, stated as a yearly rate which includes such items as interest, mortgage insurance, and certain points or credit costs

6.   Lenders will typically negotiate a modification that enables the homeowner to obtain a fully amortized, fixed rate loan.

7.   Refinancing is the act a new loan in order to pay off the existing mortgage or to gain access to the existing equity in the home.

8.   B. A snapshot of minimum requirements

9.   A decline in the value of a property as opposed to appreciation

10.   The lowering of an interest rate, extension of an amortization term, and method of amortization applied to the loan balance may all have a dramatic effect on the homeowner's ability to resume making timely payments against the mortgage note.

Loss Mitigation Answer Key #7

Name: _____

Date: _____

Score: _____

Instructor: _____

1. In order to be a viable option, each workout option will have specific qualifications that the homeowner, the property, and the lender must meet.

2. The sales comparison approach assesses the characteristics of the subject property as compared to other similar properties sold within a given time period.

3. FALSE - The traditional refinance option is typically employed with those homeowners who contact the loss mitigation department before a default situation exists.

4. Loan-to-Value Ratio is the ratio of a mortgage loan amount to the property's appraised value or selling price, whichever is less For example, if a home is sold for $100,000 and the mortgage amount is $80,000 the LTV is 80%

5. TRUE – A product matrix is a snapshot of the minimum requirements needed to place a loan in a particular approval tier or level. You can easily complete a preliminary screening of the homeowner criteria using the product matrix.

6. A home inspection is an inspection by a building professional that evaluates the structural and mechanical condition of a property.

7. FALSE – A homeowner would not qualify for a short sale workout if they have simply chosen the surrender option and do not meet the qualifying criteria of need set forth by the lender.

8. property condition
    sales price
    any other information deemed applicable

9. TRUE – The short sale approval and sales price basis will be dependent on the appraisal completed on the property.

10. An appraised value is the opinion of a property's fair market value, based on an appraiser's inspection and analysis of the property.

Name:
_____

Date:
_____

Score:
_____

Instructor:
_____

1.   FALSE - A deed in lieu of foreclosure dictates that the homeowner executes a deed that relinquishes their interest in the property to the lender in exchange for a satisfaction of the mortgage. The lender then offers the property for sale in the general market.

2.   To validate a document.

3.   Most lenders will require that the homeowner complete necessary cosmetic repairs to the property and may reject a short sale option of the property requires extensive or costly structural or other repair work to bring it up to market standards.

4.   The order by a court as to money owed or other definitive decisions.

5.   b. false: A general lien may affect any real estate owned by the individual who is the subject of the lien.

6.   Depreciation is a decline in the value of a property as opposed to appreciation

7.   Liens may be imposed against fixtures, improvements, and real property.

8.   Equity is the value of a homeowner's unencumbered interest in real estate. Equity is the difference between the homes fair market value and the unpaid balance of the mortgage and any outstanding liens Equity increases as the mortgage is paid down or as the property enjoys appreciation.

9.   A voluntary lien is created against a property when an owner uses it as collateral to borrower money.

10.   Job Transfer
      Divorce
      Reduced Income
      Death of One Party

Loss Mitigation Answer Key #9

1.   The initial contact is the most essential information-gathering period.

2.   A foreclosure is the legal process by which a homeowner in default on a mortgage is deprived of interest in the property This usually involves a forced sale of the property at public auction with the proceeds of the sale being applied to the mortgage debt.

3   A requirement of the short sale process is that the homeowner must show a good faith effort to sell the property.

4.   A title that is clear of liens, encumbrances and other defects.

5.   FALSE – The pre-foreclosure loss mitigation process enables the homeowner to relinquish the property and negotiate to remove any accountability for any sale shortfalls that may result from the sale of the property in the current market.

6.   The housing expense is the percentage of gross monthly income that goes toward paying a Ratio mortgage or rent on a home.

7.   Loss mitigation negotiations opens up the possibility of multiple intervention techniques designed to prevent foreclosure.

8.   The note is the document giving evidence of mortgage indebtedness, including the amount and terms of repayment.

9.   A short sale approval dictates that the homeowner offer the property for sale to the general market. During the sale process, the property owner must maintain the property and do everything within their power to market the property and facilitate a sale.

10.   Loan modification is a process where the lender and homeowner agree on new mortgage terms that are acceptable to both parties.

Name:

Date:

Score:

Instructor:

1.   FALSE – A short sale is often termed a pre-foreclosure sale.

2.   A acceleration clause is the section of a mortgage document that allows the lender to speed up the payment date in the event of default, making the entire principal amount due.

3.   TRUE - In a pre-foreclosure sale, the lender agrees to accept the proceeds of a sale set a current fair market value as indicated by comparables and appraisals for the market of the property.

4.   A lis pendens is a pending lawsuit; in real estate, the constructive notice filed in public records that a legal dispute exists over a piece of property.

5.   The short sale option should be considered as a workout option whenever a homeowner fails to meet lesser loss mitigation workout options.

6.   A mortgage servicer organization that collects monthly mortgage principal and interest payments from homeowners and manages escrow accounts for paying taxes and homeowners' insurance premiums The servicer often services mortgages that have been purchased by an investor in the secondary mortgage market

7.   FALSE – The DIL dictates that the homeowner will surrender possession of the property promptly, provide the lender with a deed transferring any and all interest held by the homeowner, and leave the property in good, marketable condition.

8.   A homeowner may negotiate the payment of a stipulated amount of cash from the lender in exchange for leaving the property in broom clean condition (as is standard for traditional property transfers) and for vacating the property in a timely manner.

9.   When a property is sold by order of the court is it termed a foreclosure.

10.   The theory behind the property condition requirements are that many homeowners will be unable or unwilling to resume regular payments on a property whose

condition is greatly deteriorated or whose value is exponentially lower than the mortgage principal balance.

Name: _____

Date: _____

Score: _____

Instructor: _____

1.   A quitclaim deed contains no warranties, covenants, or even the promise that the individual signing the deed holds any interest in the property.

2.   An underwriter is a company or person undertaking the responsibility for issuing a mortgage. Underwriters analyze a homeowner's credit worthiness and set the loan amount.

3.   A cession deed is a form of Quitclaim Deed.

4.   A forbearance plan enables the homeowner who has suffered a temporary financial setback that has a definitive end to halt making monthly payments or reduce the monthly payment amount until the end of the financial hardship. This plan enables the lender to begin receive full principal and interest payments from the homeowner a the end of the financial hardship.

5.   A deed restriction may limit the actions of any party gaining ownership or other interest in a property.

6.   An Amortization Schedule is a timetable for the gradual repayment of a mortgage loan. An amortization schedule indicates the amount of each payment applied to interest and principal, and the remaining balance after each payment is made.

7.   The first step in the loss mitigation process is to screen the homeowners profile to isolate potential intervention options.

Calculation Exercises

DEBT-TO-INCOME RATIO EXERCISES

To calculate a borrower's debt to income take the total monthly debt load and divide it by the total monthly income. For example:

A borrower who earns $2800.00 monthly and has installment debt of $750.00 monthly has a debt-to-income ratio of 26.78%.

D   I   R
750 / 2800 = 26.78%

1.   Income $6200
      Debt $1900

      _____
      Ratio   %

2.   Income $3000
      Debt $1350

      _____
      Ratio   %

3.   Income $3750
      Debt $ 970

      _____
      Ratio   %

4.   Income $1600
      Debt $ 340

      _____
      Ratio   %

5.   Income $2000
      Debt $ 420

      _____
      Ratio   %

6.   Income $2480
      Debt $ 920

      _____
      Ratio   %

7.   Income $4200
      Debt $1850

      _____
      Ratio   %

8.   Income $4800
      Debt $2175

      _____
      Ratio   %

9. Income $5100
Debt $1950

Ratio _____ %

10. Income $5500
Debt $1775

Ratio _____ %

11. Income $5750
Debt $1900

Ratio _____ %

12. Income $3425
Debt $1350

Ratio _____ %

13. Income $4387
Debt $1218

Ratio _____ %

14. Income $2330
Debt $ 961

Ratio _____ %

POST-FORBEARANCE PAYMENT

Use the mortgage payment to calculate a forbearance payment that requires the homeowner to repay arrearages at ½ times the regularly stipulated payment.

Mortgage	+	½ Mortgage	=	Post-Forbearance Payment
$750	+	$375	=	$1126

1. Mortgage Repayment $1900

2. Mortgage Repayment $1350

3. Mortgage Repayment $970

4. Mortgage Repayment $340

5. Mortgage Repayment $420

6. Mortgage Repayment $920

7. Mortgage Repayment $1850

8. Mortgage Repayment $2175

9. Mortgage Repayment $1950

10. Mortgage Repayment $1775

11. Mortgage Repayment $1200

12. Mortgage Repayment $1650

13. Mortgage Repayment $1218

14. Mortgage Repayment $961

POST-FORBEARANCE PAYMENT

Use the mortgage payment and post forbearance arrearages payment to calculate the potential post forbearance front end DTI.

Mortgage	+	½ Mortgage	=	Post-Forbearance Payment
$750	+	$375	=	$1126

Total Payment	/	Income	=	Repayment Ratio
$750	/	$2800	=	26.78%

1. Mortgage $1900
    Repayment   + _____

    Income $6200
    Ratio   ____ %

2. Mortgage $1350
    _____   Repayment + ____

    _____   Income $5000
    Ratio   ____ %

3. Mortgage $970
    Repayment   + _____

    Income $3750
    Ratio   ____ %

4. Mortgage $340
    Repayment   + ____

    _____   Income $1600
    Ratio   ____ %

5.   Mortgage $420
       Repayment   + _____

       Income $2000_____
       Ratio   ____%

6.   Mortgage $920
       _____ Repayment   + _____

       _____ Income $2480
       Ratio   ____%

7.   Mortgage $1850
       Repayment   + _____

       Income $4200_____
       Ratio   ____%

8.   Mortgage $2175
       Repayment   + _____

       _____ Income $4800
       Ratio   ____%

9.   Mortgage $1950
       Repayment   + _____

       Income $5100_____
       Ratio   ____%

10.   Mortgage $1775
       Repayment   + ____

       _____ Income $5500
       Ratio   ____%

11.   Mortgage $1900
        Repayment   + _____

        Income $5750
        Ratio   %

12.   Mortgage $1350
        Repayment   + _____

        Income $3425
        Ratio   %

13.   Mortgage $1218
        Repayment   + _____

        Income $4387
        Ratio   %

14.   Mortgage $961
        Repayment   + _____

        Income $2330
        Ratio   %

BACK-END DEBT

Calculate the back end debt ratio.

Mortgage	+	Monthly Payment	=	Debt Load
$900	+	$300	=	$200

Debt Load	/	Income	=	DTI
$1200	/	$3000	=	40%

1. Mortgage $1900
    + Other Debt $1300

    / Income $5700
    = Ratio

2. Mortgage $ 800
    + Other Debt $ 556

    / Income $3150
    = Ratio

3. Mortgage $ 428
    + Other Debt $ 220

    / Income $1670
    = Ratio

4. Mortgage $ 556
    + Other Debt $ 353

    / Income $2800
    = Ratio

5.   Mortgage $2850
      + Other Debt $1200

      / Income $7500
      = Ratio

6.   Mortgage $1155
      + Other Debt $ 875

      / Income $4800
      = Ratio

7.   Mortgage $2100
      + Other Debt $1100

      / Income $6000
      = Ratio

8.   Mortgage $ 510
      + Other Debt $285

      / Income $2250
      = Ratio

9.   Mortgage $ 800
      + Other Debt $200

      / Income $3890
      = Ratio

10.   Mortgage $1255
      + Other Debt $1060

      / Income $5575
      = Ratio

MODIFICATION CALCULATION

Calculate the payment difference for each of the rate modifications in the chart.

Loan Amount	Interest Rate 10.375 30-year Amortization	Interest Rate 6.250 30-year Amortization	Payment Difference
$100,000	$ 905.41	$ 614.72	
$125,000	$1131.76	$ 769.65	
$150.000	$1358.11	$ 923.58	
$175,000	$1584.76	$1077.51	
$200,000	$1810.81	$1231.43	
$225,000	$2037.17	$1385.36	

Calculate the old and new Front End Ratio

Income	Interest Rate 10.375 30-year Amortization	Pre-Modification DTI	Interest Rate 6.250 30-year Amortization	Post-Modification DTI
$4175	$ 905.41		$ 614.72	
$4175	$1131.76		$ 769.65	
$4175	$1358.11		$ 923.58	
$7200	$1584.76		$1077.51	
$7200	$1810.81		$1231.43	
$$7200	$2037.17		$1385.36	

SAMPLE RATE SHEET

Grade	LTV	40 Year Fixed		30 Year Fixed	
		Par	<1.00>	Par	<1.00>
A 660+	97%	6.500	7.000	7.000	7.500
Mortgage 0X30	95%	6.125	6.625	6.500	7.000
Consumer 1X30	90%	6.000	6.500	6.125	6.625
BK/For 3/ 3	85%	5.875	6.125	6.000	6.500
DTI 41%	80%	5.750	6.250	5.875	6.375
	75%	5.625	6.125	5.750	6.250
B	95%	7.125	7.500	8.000	8.500
620-669	90%	7.000	7.375	7.875	8.375
Mtg 1x30	85%	6.625	7.000	7.500	8.000
Con any	80%	6.500	6.875	7.125	7.625
BK / For 3/ 3	75%	6.125	6.500	6.875	7.375
DTI 45%	70%	5.875	6.125	6.500	7.000
C	90%	7.500	8.000	8.500	
590-619	85%	7.375	7.875	8.375	
Mtg 2X60	80%	7.000	7.500	8.000	
Con any	75%	6.875	7.125	7.875	8.125
BK / For 2/ 2	70%	6.500	6.875	7.500	7.875
DTI 47%					
D	85%	7.875	8.375		
560-589	80%	7.500	8.000	8.500	
Mtg 90+	75%	7.125	7.625	8.375	
Con any	70%	6.875	7.125	8.250	
BK/ For 2/ 2					
DTI 50%					

Calculation Answer Keys

DTI Ratio Exercises		Post Forbearance Payment	
1.	30.65%	1.	$950
2.	45%	2.	$675
3.	25.6%	3.	$485
4.	21.25%	4.	$170
5.	25.87%	5.	$210
6.	30.1%	6.	$460
7.	44.05%	7.	$925
8.	45.31%	8.	$1087.50
9.	38.24%	9.	$975
10.	32.27%	10.	$887.50
11.	33%	11.	$950
12.	32.27%	12.	$675
13.	27.76%	13.	$609
14.	41.24%	14.	$480.50

Post Forbearance Payment		/	Ratio
1.	$2850		45.97%
2.	$2025		40.5%
3.	$1455		38.8%
4.	$510		31.8%
5.	$630		31.5%
6.	$1380		55.65%
7.	$2775		66.07%
8.	$3262.50		67.97%
9.	$2925		57.35%
10.	$2662.50		48.41%
11.	$2850		49.57%
12.	$2025		59.12%
13.	$1827		41.65%
14.	$1441.50		61.87%

Back End Debt Ratio
1.   56.14%
2.   39.68%
3.   38.80%
4.   32.46%
5.   54%
6.   42.19%
7.   53.33%
8.   35.33%
9.   25.70%
10.   41.52%

MODIFICATION CALCULATION

Calculate the payment difference for each of the rate modifications in the chart.

Loan Amount	Interest Rate 10.375 30-year Amortization	Interest Rate 6.250 30-year Amortization	Payment Difference
$100,000	$ 905.41	$ 614.72	$289.69
$125,000	$1131.76	$ 769.65	$362.11
$150.000	$1358.11	$ 923.58	$434.53
$175,000	$1584.76	$1077.51	$507.25
$200,000	$1810.81	$1231.43	$579.38
$225,000	$2037.17	$1385.36	$651.81

Calculate the old and new Front End Ratio

Income	Interest Rate 10.375 30-year Amortization	Pre-Modification DTI	Interest Rate 6.250 30-year Amortization	Post-Modification DTI
$4175	$ 905.41	21.69	$ 614.72	14.74
$4175	$1131.76	27.10	$ 769.65	18.43
$4175	$1358.11	32.53	$ 923.58	22.12
$7200	$1584.76	25.15	$1077.51	14.97
$7200	$1810.81	26.15	$1231.43	17.10
$$7200	$2037.17	28.29	$1385.36	19.24

Calculating LTV		Maximum PITI	
1.	$84,150	1.	$450.00
2.	$99,000	2.	$483.00
3.	$137,655	3.	$547.20
4.	$60,000	4.	$419.50
5.	$48,930	5.	$451.35
6.	$78,675	6.	$1123.75
		7.	$693.00
		8.	$266.25
		9.	$534.60
		10.	$182.50

Loss Mitigation Review Forms

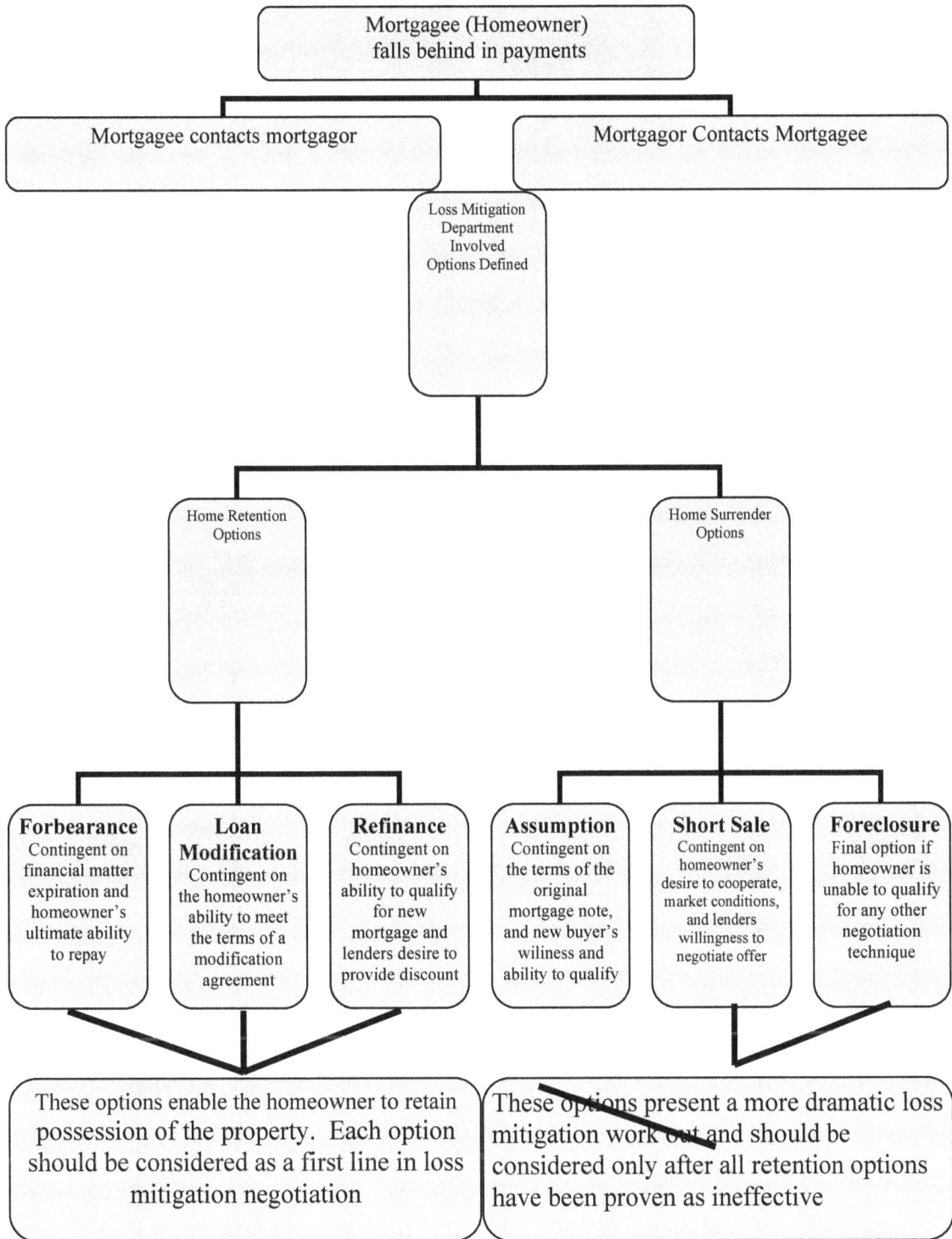

```
                  ┌─────────────────────────────┐
                  │   Mortgagee (Homeowner)     │
                  │    falls behind in payments │
                  └─────────────────────────────┘
           ┌──────────────┴───────────────┐
┌────────────────────────┐    ┌────────────────────────────┐
│ Mortgagee contacts     │    │ Mortgagor Contacts         │
│ mortgagor              │    │ Mortgagee                  │
└────────────────────────┘    └────────────────────────────┘
```

Loss Mitigation
Department
Involved
Options Defined

Home Retention
Options

Home Surrender
Options

Forbearance
Contingent on financial matter expiration and homeowner's ultimate ability to repay

Loan Modification
Contingent on the homeowner's ability to meet the terms of a modification agreement

Refinance
Contingent on homeowner's ability to qualify for new mortgage and lenders desire to provide discount

Assumption
Contingent on the terms of the original mortgage note, and new buyer's wiliness and ability to qualify

Short Sale
Contingent on homeowner's desire to cooperate, market conditions, and lenders willingness to negotiate offer

Foreclosure
Final option if homeowner is unable to qualify for any other negotiation technique

These options enable the homeowner to retain possession of the property. Each option should be considered as a first line in loss mitigation negotiation

These options present a more dramatic loss mitigation work out and should be considered only after all retention options have been proven as ineffective

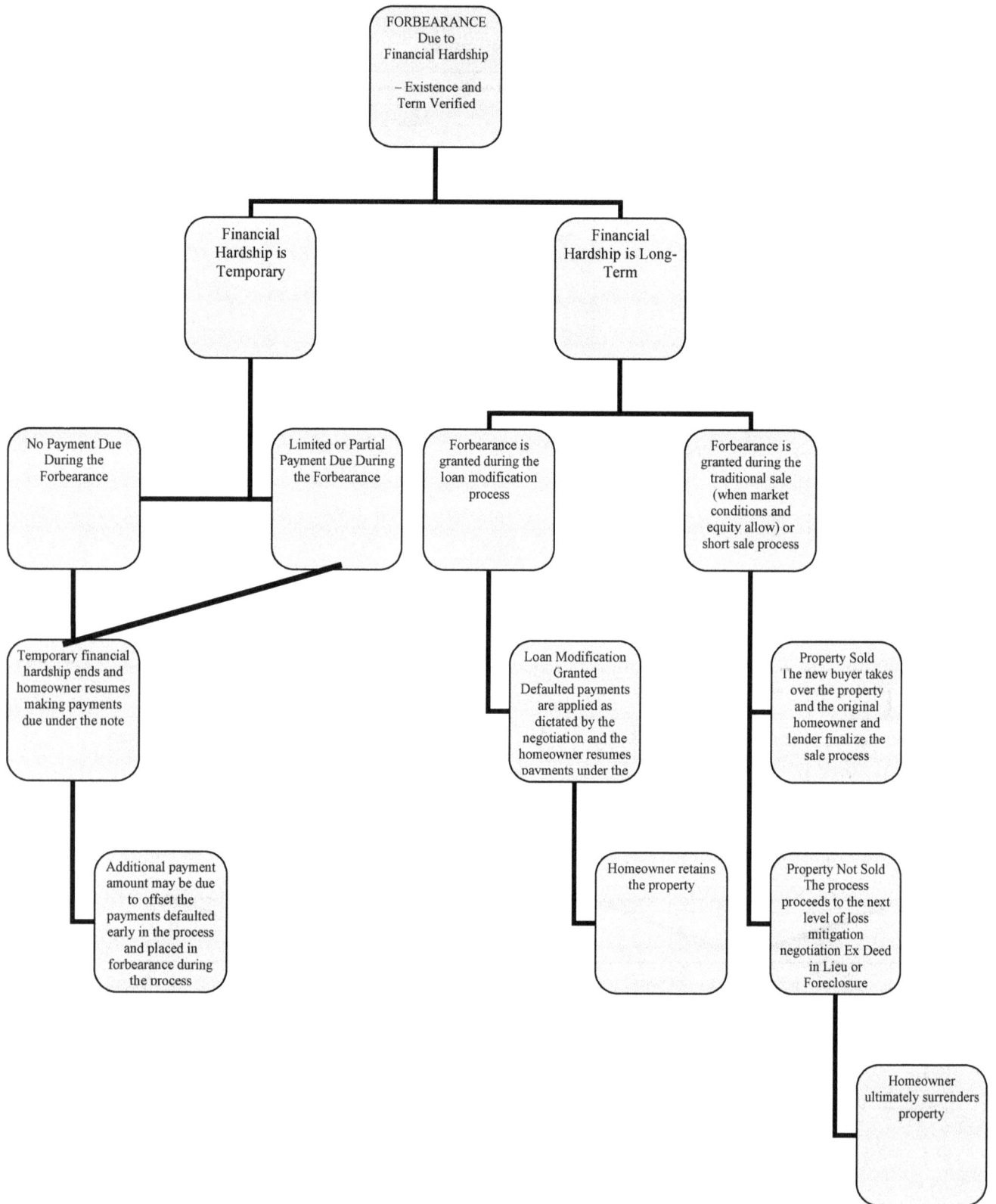

```
                         ┌──────────────────────┐
                         │      FORBEARANCE      │
                         │        Due to         │
                         │  Financial Hardship   │
                         │                       │
                         │    – Existence and    │
                         │     Term Verified     │
                         └──────────────────────┘
```

FORBEARANCE
Due to
Financial Hardship

– Existence and
Term Verified

Financial Hardship is Temporary

Financial Hardship is Long-Term

No Payment Due During the Forbearance

Limited or Partial Payment Due During the Forbearance

Forbearance is granted during the loan modification process

Forbearance is granted during the traditional sale (when market conditions and equity allow) or short sale process

Temporary financial hardship ends and homeowner resumes making payments due under the note

Loan Modification Granted
Defaulted payments are applied as dictated by the negotiation and the homeowner resumes payments under the

Property Sold
The new buyer takes over the property and the original homeowner and lender finalize the sale process

Additional payment amount may be due to offset the payments defaulted early in the process and placed in forbearance during the process

Homeowner retains the property

Property Not Sold
The process proceeds to the next level of loss mitigation negotiation Ex Deed in Lieu or Foreclosure

Homeowner ultimately surrenders property

SPECIAL FORBEARANCE INTERVIEW AND FILE CHECKLIST

Homeowner: _____

Requirement	Verification (Date, Amount, Source of Information etc.)
1. Has the homeowner experienced a verifiable loss of income or increase in living expenses?	
2. Is the term of this loss of income or increased living expense temporary?	
3. Length of expected hardship?	
4. Is the property owner occupied?	
5. Is the owner occupied status verifiable by the original mortgage application or closing occupancy declaration?	
6. Did the homeowner receive the How to Avoid Foreclosure brochure or obtain the services of a loss mitigation specialist?	
7. Will the loan be more than 90 and less than 365 days delinquent on the effective date of the agreement? (show number of days)	
8. Did the income analysis to determine the homeowner's current inability to pay the debt include:	
• A financial statement provided by the homeowner	
• A credit report	

• Income/Expense Verifications	
• Evidence the homeowner hardship is temporary	
9. Did the income analysis to determine the homeowner's ability to repay the debt after the forbearance include:	
• A financial statement provided by the homeowner	
• A credit report	
• Income/Expense Verifications	
• Evidence the homeowner can support the payment schedule	
10. The homeowner's current DTI ratio	
11. The homeowner's expected DTI ratio	
12. When and why will the homeowner's income increase?	
13. Has an inspection determined that the property has no adverse conditions affecting continued occupancy?	
14. Does the title search indicate that junior liens exist against the property?	
15. Does the homeowner's expected income support the ability to resume payments with these junior liens in place?	
16. Does the written agreement executed by the homeowner:	

• Clearly define the terms and frequency of repayment	
• Offer relief not available through a normal repayment plan	
• State that failure to comply may result in foreclosure	
• Limit the total default to 12 months or less	
17. If the special forbearance agreement culminates in a modification or short sale, has the proposed type and date of the action been negotiated?	

Figure 2:2 Forbearance Sample Form – File Checklist
This form is included for reference purposes only. You should obtain the applicable HUD or Lender forms for use in a negotiation.

LOAN MODIFICATION CHECKLIST

Homeowner: _____

Requirement	Verification (Date, Amount, Source of Information etc.)
1. Has the homeowner experienced a verifiable loss of income or increase in living expenses?	
2. Is the term of the loss if income or increased living expense temporary or long term?	
3. Is the increased living expense a result of a change in the interest rate of an adjustable rate loan?	
4. Does the homeowner have a commitment to continue to occupy the property as his or her primary residence?	
5. Is the owner occupied status verifiable by the original mortgage application or closing occupancy declaration?	
6. Did the homeowner receive the How to Avoid Foreclosure brochure?	
7. Will the loan be more than 90 days delinquent on the date of execution and funding? (show number of days)?	
8. Did the income analysis to determine the homeowner's current inability ability to repay the debt include:	
• A financial statement provided by the homeowner	
• A credit report	

• Income/expense verifications	
9. What is the pre-modification DTI?	
10. Post-modification DTI?	
11. Why can't the default be cured by a special forbearance arrangement?	
12. Has a property appraisal been completed to determine the current market value of the property?	
13. Current Market Value	
14. Has an inspection determined that the property has no adverse conditions affecting the continued occupancy?	
15. Has a title search established first lien status of the modified loan?	
• Will release of junior liens be required	
• Will title endorsement be required	
16. Does the homeowner's DTI Assessment support the ability to maintain the modified payment with the junior liens in place?	
17. Does the written modification agreement executed by the homeowner:	
• Include all advances necessary to reinstate the principal, interest, taxes and insurance?	
• Exclude all legal and administrative costs?	
• Define the terms of the newly modified note?	

• Offer relief not available through a normal repayment plan?	
• State that failure to comply with the terms of the modified note may result in foreclosure.	

Figure 3:6 Sample Modification Checklist
This form is included for reference purposes only. You should obtain the applicable HUD or Lender forms for use in a negotiation

SAMPLE PROCESS OF A SHORT SALE

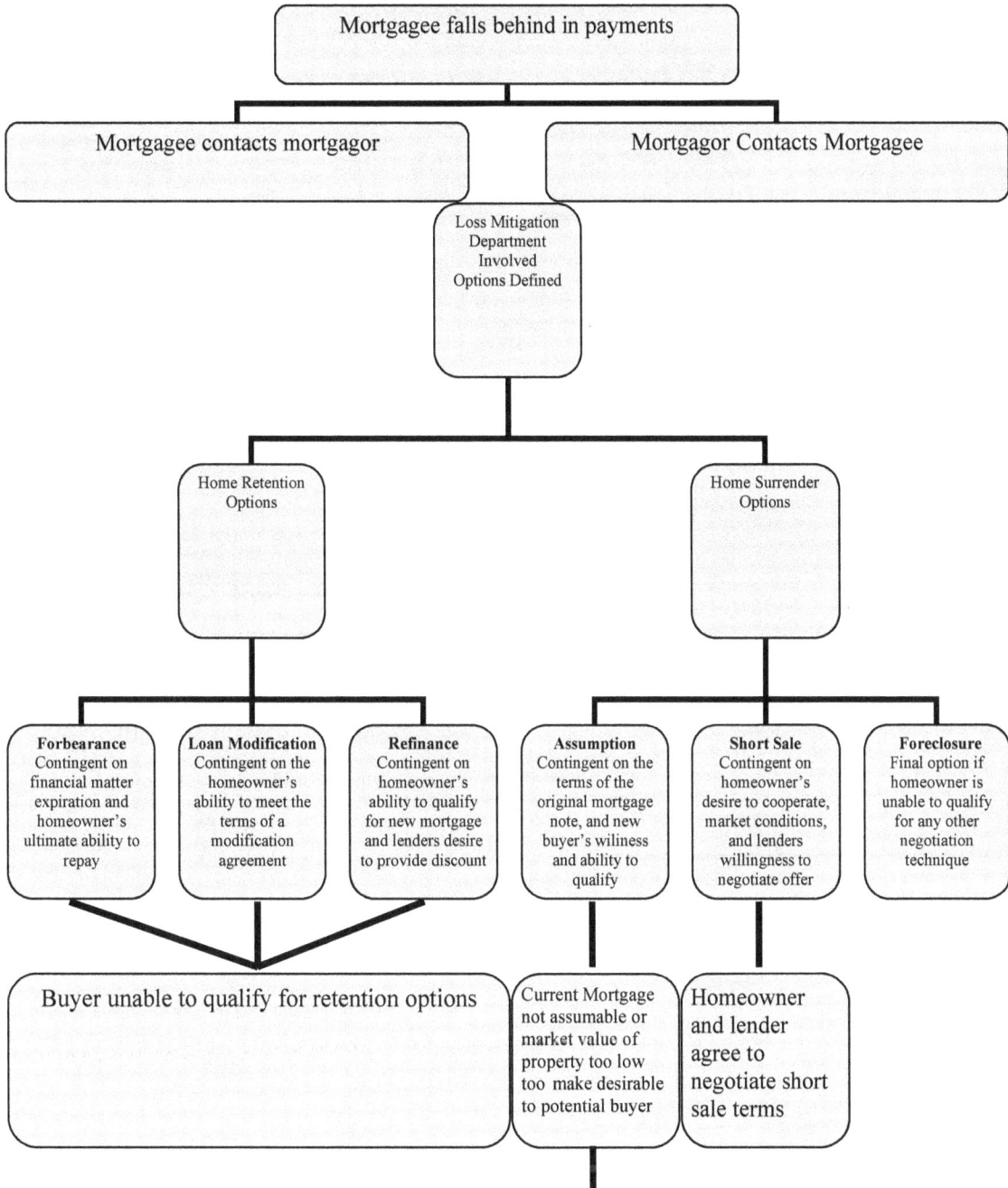

Mortgagee falls behind in payments

Mortgagee contacts mortgagor

Mortgagor Contacts Mortgagee

Loss Mitigation
Department
Involved
Options Defined

Home Retention
Options

Home Surrender
Options

Forbearance
Contingent on
financial matter
expiration and
homeowner's
ultimate ability to
repay

Loan Modification
Contingent on the
homeowner's
ability to meet the
terms of a
modification
agreement

Refinance
Contingent on
homeowner's
ability to qualify
for new mortgage
and lenders desire
to provide discount

Assumption
Contingent on the
terms of the
original mortgage
note, and new
buyer's wiliness
and ability to
qualify

Short Sale
Contingent on
homeowner's
desire to cooperate,
market conditions,
and lenders
willingness to
negotiate offer

Foreclosure
Final option if
homeowner is
unable to qualify
for any other
negotiation
technique

Buyer unable to qualify for retention options

Current Mortgage
not assumable or
market value of
property too low
too make desirable
to potential buyer

Homeowner
and lender
agree to
negotiate short
sale terms

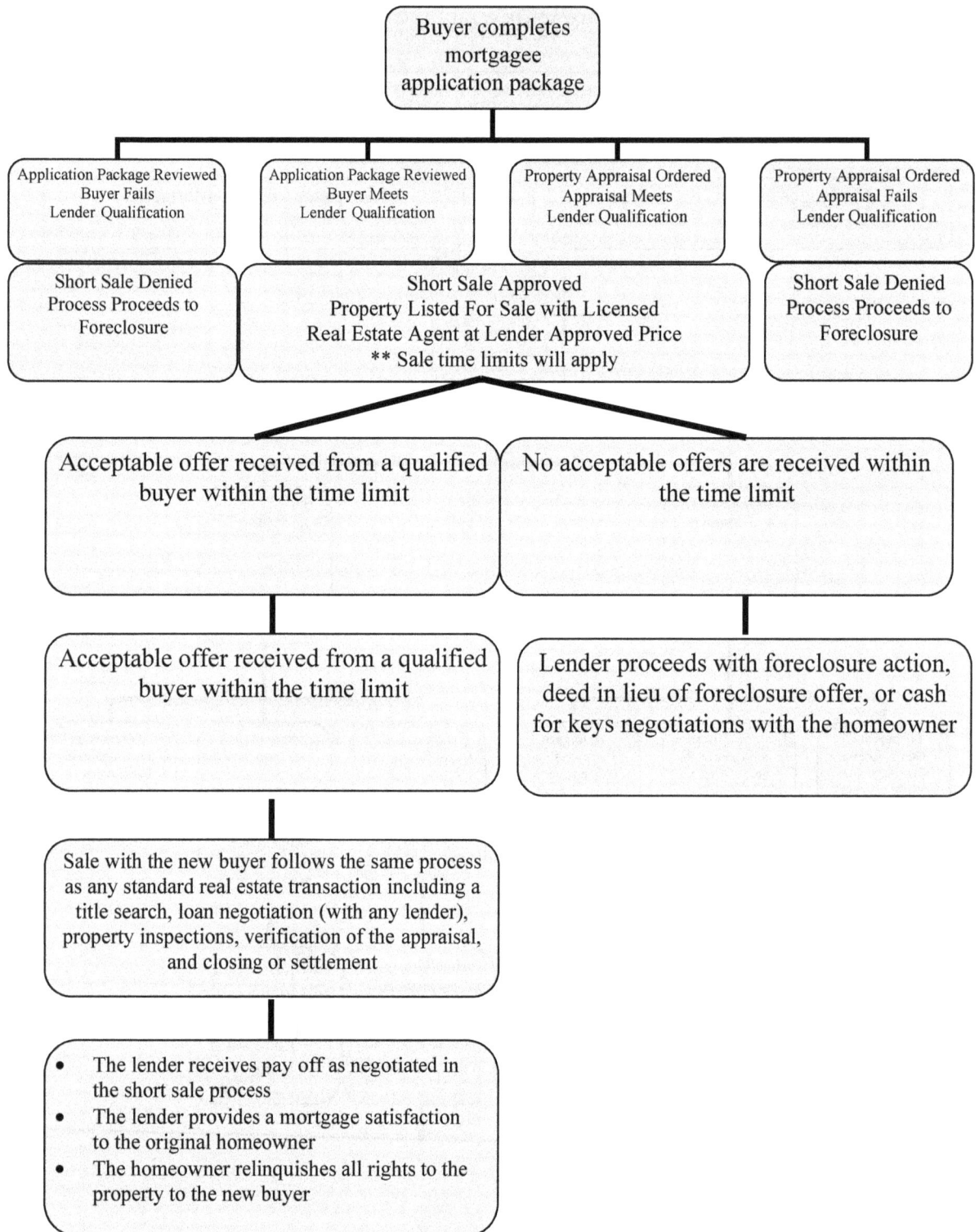

```
                    ┌─────────────────────┐
                    │   Buyer completes   │
                    │     mortgagee       │
                    │ application package │
                    └─────────────────────┘
```

| Application Package Reviewed Buyer Fails Lender Qualification | Application Package Reviewed Buyer Meets Lender Qualification | Property Appraisal Ordered Appraisal Meets Lender Qualification | Property Appraisal Ordered Appraisal Fails Lender Qualification |

| Short Sale Denied Process Proceeds to Foreclosure | Short Sale Approved Property Listed For Sale with Licensed Real Estate Agent at Lender Approved Price ** Sale time limits will apply | Short Sale Denied Process Proceeds to Foreclosure |

| Acceptable offer received from a qualified buyer within the time limit | No acceptable offers are received within the time limit |

| Acceptable offer received from a qualified buyer within the time limit | Lender proceeds with foreclosure action, deed in lieu of foreclosure offer, or cash for keys negotiations with the homeowner |

Sale with the new buyer follows the same process as any standard real estate transaction including a title search, loan negotiation (with any lender), property inspections, verification of the appraisal, and closing or settlement

- The lender receives pay off as negotiated in the short sale process
- The lender provides a mortgage satisfaction to the original homeowner
- The homeowner relinquishes all rights to the property to the new buyer

SHORT SALE (PFS) CHECKLIST

Homeowner: _____

Requirement	Verification (Date, Amount, Source of Information etc.)
1. Has the homeowner experienced a verifiable loss of income or increase in living expenses?	
2. Is the term of this loss of income or increased living expense temporary or long term?	
3. Length of expected hardship?	
4. Has the homeowner worked with a loss mitigation specialist to qualify for lesser/retention loss mitigation options?	
5. Why is a special forbearance not applicable?	
6. Why is a loan modification not applicable?	
7. Why is a short refinance not applicable?	
8. Is the property owner occupied?	
9. Is the owner occupied status verifiable by the original mortgage application or closing occupancy declaration?	
10. Did the homeowner receive the How to Avoid Foreclosure brochure or obtain the services of a loss mitigation specialist?	
11. Will the loan be at least 30 days delinquent when the transaction closes? (show number of days)	

12. Did the income analysis to determine the homeowner's current inability to pay the debt include:	
• A financial statement provided by the homeowner	
• A credit report	
• Income/Expense Verifications	
• Evidence the homeowner hardship is long-term	
• Evidence the homeowner does not qualify for lesser/retention work out options	
13. The homeowner's current DTI ratio	
14. The homeowner's expected DTI ratio	
15. Does an appraisal show that:	
• The AS IS value is less than the loan amount? (show Value)	
• The property is worth at least 63% of the unpaid principal balance. (show negative equity ratio)	
• sale proceeds will result in a loss of more than $1,000	
• The property is not seriously damaged. •	
16. Has a title search been obtained indicating marketable title?	

17. Does the title search indicate that junior liens exist against the property?	
18. Can these liens be discharged?	
19. Can these liens be paid/negotiated?	
20. Does the short sale agreement, executed by the homeowner	
• Define end date for marketing	
• State the minimum acceptable net proceeds	
• Define the methods of termination of agreement	
• Outline the homeowner good faith responsibilities	
• Offer relief not available through a retention loss mitigation option	
• State that failure to comply may result in foreclosure	
• State that the receipt and closing of an acceptable offer will result in a satisfaction of the original note	
21. Do Net Sale proceeds equal or exceed 82% of As Is Value? (show %)	

Figure 5:1 Sample Short Sale Checklist
This form is included for reference purposes only. You should obtain the applicable HUD or Lender forms for use in a negotiation.

DEED-IN-LIEU OF FORECLOSURE CHECKLIST

Homeowner: _____

Requirement	Verification (Date, Amount, Source of Information etc.)
1. Has the homeowner experienced a verifiable loss of income or increase in living expenses?	
2. Is the term of this loss of income or increased living expense temporary?	
3. Is the property owner occupied?	
4. Is the owner occupied status verifiable by the original mortgage application or closing occupancy declaration?	
5. If the property is other than owner occupied, what exceptions qualify this property for DIL negotiations?	
6. Did the homeowner receive the How to Avoid Foreclosure brochure or obtain the services of a loss mitigation specialist?	
7. Will the loan be at least 30 days delinquent when the special warranty deed is accepted?	
8. Did the income analysis to determine the homeowner's current inability to pay the debt include:	
• A financial statement provided by the homeowner	
• A credit report	

• Income/Expense Verifications	
• Evidence the homeowner hardship is long-term	
9. The homeowner's current DTI ratio	
10. A recent appraisal indicates the AS IS property value is	
11. If any portion of the property is rented, is occupied conveyance approved?	
12. Has a title search been obtained showing good and marketable title?	
13. If junior liens exist, will these be discharged prior to transfer?	
14. Does a written DIL agreement, executed by the homeowner:	
• Require the property to be vacant and free of personal property at conveyance?	
• Convey title via a special warranty deed?	
• Convey clear title free of junior liens?	
• Require the homeowner to pay utility bills to the date of conveyance?	
• Require the homeowner to pay HOA dues or other assessments?	
• Advise the homeowner to obtain the advice of a tax consultant?	

• State that failure to comply may result in foreclosure	

Figure 2:2 DIL File Checklist
This form is included for reference purposes only. You should obtain the applicable
HUD or Lender forms for use in a negotiation.

Assessment Questionnaire Date: _____

Source: Homeowner Contact _____   Lender Referral _____   Other: _____

Homeowner Name: _____   Co-Homeowner Name: _____

Home Phone: _____   Other Phone: _____   Best time(s) to call: _____

Explanation of Default/Notes: _____

_____

_____

_____

DOB: _____ SSN: _____   DOB: _____ SSN: _____

May I run a credit report? ___ Yes ___ No   May I run a credit report? ___ Yes ___ No

Are you behind in any other debt? _____

_____

Property Address: _____

Is this your primary residence? __ Yes __ No   Have you lived there since the original purchase? __ Yes __ No

No. Yrs: __   Current Value $_____   Value at Purchase $_____   Mortgage Balance $_____

Missed Payments #____   Amount Each Payment $ _____   Partial Payments: _____

Have you discussed the situation with the lender?   __ Yes __ No   Results _____

Are you presently Employed? __ Yes __ No   Are you presently Employed? _ Yes _ No

If No Reason: _____   If No Reason: _____

Term: _____   Term: _____

Employer: _____   Employer: _____

Address: _____   Address: _____

Phone: _____ No yrs. __ Position: _____   Phone. _____ No yrs. __ Position: _____

Explanation of Employment/Notes: _____

_____

_____

_____

Figure 7:1 Sample Assessment Form – Page 1
This form is included for reference purposes only. You should obtain the applicable HUD or Lender forms for use in a negotiation.

PRESENT Income

Homeowners Mthly $_____

           Prev Year $_____

Co-Homeowners Mthly $_____

           Prev Year $_____

Other Income _____ $_____

Other Income _____ $_____

    Total Income Current $_____

EXPECTED Income – Date _____

Homeowners Mthly $_____

           Prev Year $_____

Co-Homeowners Mthly $_____

           Prev Year $_____

Other Income _____ $_____

Other Income _____ $_____

    Total Income Expected $_____

PRESENT Debt

Mortgage	$_____	Mortgage	$_____
Auto 1	$_____	Auto 1	$_____
Auto 2	$_____	Auto 2	$_____
Revolving 1	$_____	Revolving 1	$_____
Revolving 2	$_____	Revolving 2	$_____
Other _____	$_____	Other _____	$_____
Other _____	$_____	Other _____	$_____

    Total Debt Current $_____   Total Debt Expected $_____

    Present DTI% _____   Expected DTI %_____ (current mortgage)

Analysis:

Current DTI _____   Expected DTI _____   Date _____   Notes: _____

Surplus Income Current   _____   Surplus Income Future   _____

Current Default # Days   _____   Current Default Base Amount _____

Owner Occ ___ Yes ___ No If No Exception Reason   _____

Est Payoff _____   Orig Mtg _____   Orig Value _____ Est Value _____

Forbearance Analysis: Term of Hardship _____   Current DTI _____   Expected DTI _____

    Surplus Income Present _____   Surplus Income Present _____

    Required Term _____   Forbearance Pmt Amt _____

    Post Forbearance Pmt Add On_____

Figure 7:2 Sample Assessment Form – Page 2
This form is included for reference purposes only. You should obtain the applicable HUD or Lender forms for use in a negotiation.

Modification Analysis:

Rate Change #1 _____   New Pmt _____   DTI _____

Rate Change #2 _____   New Pmt _____   DTI _____

Rate #1 + Term Mod 30   New Pmt _____

Rate #2 + Term Mod 40   New Pmt _____

Possible Principal Reduction   _____

Red + Rate #1 + Term 30   New Pmt _____

Red + Rate #2 + Term 40   New Pmt _____

Qualification Analysis: _____

Refi Pos ____ Yes ____ No Notes _____

Referral _____   Date _____

Short Sale Analysis:

Orig Value $_____   Orig Note $_____   Pres Value $_____   Pres Principal _____

SP / Value _____

Prop Condition Notes: _____

Analysis Notes: _____

Figure 7:3 Sample Assessment Form – Page 3
This form is included for reference purposes only. You should obtain the applicable HUD or Lender forms for use in a negotiation.

REQUEST FOR VERIFICATION OF DEPOSIT

Privacy Act Notice: This information is to be used by the agency collecting it or its assignees in determining whether you qualify as a prospective mortgagor under its program. It will not be disclosed outside the agency except as required and permitted by law. You do not have to provide this information, but if you do not your application for approval as a prospective mortgagor or borrower may be delayed or rejected. The information requested in this form is authorized by Title 38, USC. Chapter 37 (if VA); by 12 USC, Section 1701 et. Seq (if HUD/FHA); by 42 USC, Section 1452b (if HUD/CPD); and Title 42 USC, 1471 et. Seq., or 7 USC. 1971 et. Deq. (if USDA/FmHA).

Instructions	Lender – Complete items 1 through 8. Have applicant complete item 9. Forward directly to depository named in item 1.
	Depository – Please complete Items 10 through 18 and return DIRECTLY to lender named in item 2.
	This form is to be transmitted directly to the lender and is not to be transmitted through the applicant or any other party.

PART I - REQUEST

1. To (Name and address of depository)	2. From (Name and address of Lender)

I certify that this verification has been sent directly to the bank or depository and ahs not passed through the hands of the applicant or any other interested party.

2. Signature of Lender	4. Title	4. Date	6. Lender's Number (Optional)

7. Information To Be Verified

Type of Account	Account in Name of	Account Number	Balance
			$
			$
			$

To Depository: I/We have applied for a mortgage loan and stated in my financial statement that the balance on deposit with you is as shown above. You are authorized to verify this information and to supply the lender identified above with the information requested in Items 10 through 13. Your response is solely a matter of courtesy for which no responsibility is attached to your institution or any of your officers.

8. Name and Address of Applicant(s)	9. Signature of Applicant(s)

PART II – VERIFICATION OF DEPOSITORY To Be Completed By Depository

10. Deposit Accounts of Applicant(s)

Type of Account	Account in Name of	Account Number	Balance
			$
			$
			$

11. Loans Outstanding To Applicants

Loan Number	Date of Loan	Original Amount	Current Balance	Installments (Monthly/Quarterly)		Secured By	Number of Late Payments
		$	$	$	per		
		$	$	$	per		
		$	$	$	per		

12. Please include any additional information which may be of assistance in determination of credit worthiness. (Please include information on loans paid-in-full in Item 11 above)

13. If the name(s) on the account(s) differ from those listed in Item 7, please supply the name(s) on the account(s) as reflected by your records.

PART III – Authorized Signature – Federal statutes provide severe penalty for any fraud, intentional misrepresentation, or criminal connivance or conspiracy purposed to influence the issuance of any guaranty or insurance by the VA Secretary, the U.S.D.A., FmHA/FHA Commissioner, or the HUD/CPD Assistant Secretary.

14. Signature of Depository Representative	15. Title (please print or type)	16. Date
17. Please print or type name signed in item 14	18. Phone No.	

Figure7:4 - Sample Form – VOD – HUD Release

REQUEST FOR VERIFICATION OF EMPLOYMENT

Instructions   Lender – Complete items 1 through 7. Have applicant complete item 8. Forward directly to employer named in item 1.
Employer – Please complete either Part II or Part III as applicable. Complete Part IV and return directly to lender named in item 2.
This form is to be transmitted directly to the lender and is not to be transmitted through the applicant or any other party.

Part I – Request

1. To (Name and address of employer)	2. From (Name and address of Lender)		

I certify that this verification has been sent directly to the employer and ahs not passed through the hands of the applicant or any other interested party.

2. Signature of Lender	4. Title	4. Date	6. Lender's Number (Optional)

I have applied for a mortgage loan and stated that I am now or was formerly employed by you. My signature below authorizes verification of this information.

7. Name and Address of Applicant (include employee or badge number)	8. Signature of Applicant

Part II – Verification of Present Employment

9. Applicant's Date of Employment	10. Present Position	11. Probability of Continued Employment

12A. Current Gross Base Pay (enter Amount and Check Period)
__ Annual   __ Hourly
__ Monthly   __ Other (specify)
$ _____ __ Weekly

13 For Military Personnel Only	
Pay Grade	
Type	Monthly Amount
Base Pay	$

14. If Overtime or Bonus is Applicable Is Its Continuance Likely?
Overtime   __ Yes __ No
Bonus   __ Yes __ No

15. If paid hourly – average hours per week

Type	Year to Date	Past Year 20_	Past Year 20_		
				Rations	$
Base Pay	$	$	$	Flight or Hazard	$
Overtime	$	$	$	Clothing	$
				Quarters	$
Commissions	$	$	$	Pro Pay	$
Bonus	$	$	$	Overseas or Combat	$
Total	$	$	$	Variable Housing Allowance	$

16. Date of applicant's next pay increase

17. Projected amount of next pay increase

18. Date of applicant's last pay increase

19. Amount of last pay increase

20. Remarks (If employee was off work for any length of time, please indicate time period and reason)

Part III Verification of Previous Employment

21. Date Hired	23. Salary/Wage at Termination Per (Year) (Month) (Week)
22. Date Terminated	Base _____ Overtime _____ Commissions _____ Bonus _____
24. Reason for Leaving	25. Position Held

Part IV – Authorized Signature

26. Signature of Employer	27. Title (please print or type)	28. Date
29. Print or type named signed in item 26	30. Phone No.	

Figure7:5 - Sample Form – VOE – HUD Release

DEBT TO INCOME RATIO (DTI%)

Monthly Income

Homeowner   Co-Homeowner

$_____ Base Pay/ _____ $_____ Base Pay/ _____

$_____ Commission/ _____ $_____ Commission/ _____

$_____ Other _____ $_____ Other _____

$_____ Other _____ $_____ Other _____

$_____ Total Monthly Income $_____ Total Monthly Income

Combined Current Monthly Income $_____

Income Notes: _____

Define any income adjustments that apply, the reason for these adjustments, and the duration of the applicable adjustment. Provide date of income change.

Adjusted Monthly Income: Date of Adjustment: _____ Reason: _____

Homeowner   Co-Homeowner

$_____ Base Pay/ _____ $_____ Base Pay/ _____

$_____ Commission/ _____ $_____ Commission/ _____

$_____ Other _____ $_____ Other _____

$_____ Other _____ $_____ Other _____

$_____ Total Expected Monthly Income $_____ Total Expected Monthly

Combined Adjusted Monthly Income $_____

Figure7:6 - Sample Form – DTI – Page 1

Current Monthly Debt

Homeowner

$_____ House/Rent Payment

$_____ Automobile Payment

$_____ Credit Card _____

$_____ Credit Card _____

$_____ Credit Card _____

$_____ Personal Loan _____

$_____ Other_____

$_____ Other_____

$_____ Total Monthly Debt

Co-Homeowner

$_____ House/Rent Payment

$_____ Automobile Payment

$_____ Credit Card _____

$_____ Credit Card _____

$_____ Credit Card _____

$_____ Personal Loan _____

$_____ Other_____

$_____ Other_____

$_____ Total Monthly Debt

Combined Current Monthly Debt $_____

Debt Notes: _____

Define any debt adjustments that apply, the reason for these adjustments, and the duration of the applicable adjustment. Provide date of debt change.

Adjusted Monthly Debt: Date of Adjustment: _____   Reason: _____

Adjusted Monthly Debt

Homeowner

$_____ House/Rent Payment

$_____ Automobile Payment

$_____ Credit Card _____

$_____ Credit Card _____

$_____ Credit Card _____

$_____ Personal Loan _____

$_____ Other_____

$_____ Other_____

$_____ Total Monthly Debt

Co-Homeowner

$_____ House/Rent Payment

$_____ Automobile Payment

$_____ Credit Card _____

$_____ Credit Card _____

$_____ Credit Card _____

$_____ Personal Loan _____

$_____ Other_____

$_____ Other_____

$_____ Total Monthly Debt

Combined Adjusted Monthly Debt $_____

Figure7:7 - Sample Form – DTI – Page 2

Forbearance Calculations

Current DTI Calculations

Take the total debt $_____ (factor each debt only once – if it is a joint debt list under the primary income earner only) and divide by the current combined income $_____ the total is the current DTI.

Debt _____ / Current Income _____ = Current DTI _____%

Future Calculations

Take the total debt $_____ and divide by the Future / Expected combined income $_____ the total is the expected DTI.

Debt _____ / Future Income _____ = Expected DTI _____%

Modification Calculation

Current Calculations

Add all liabilities EXCEPT mortgage _____ divide by the combined monthly income _____ the total is the other liability DTI of the homeowner.

Take the current mortgage debt $_____ and divide by the combined monthly income _____ the total is the Front End DTI.

Current Mortgage Debt _____ / Combined Income _____ = Front End DTI _____%

Mortgage (Front End DTI)% _____ + All other Debt DTI %_____ = Back End DTI _____%

Post Modification Calculations

Add all liabilities EXCEPT mortgage _____ divide by the combined monthly income _____ the total is the other liability DTI of the homeowner.

Take the current mortgage debt $_____ and divide by the combined monthly income _____ the total is the Front End DTI.

Current Mortgage Debt _____ / Combined Income _____ = Front End DTI _____ %

Mortgage (Front End DTI)% _____ + All other Debt DTI %_____ = Back End DTI _____ %

Credit History (12 months)
Homeowner

Mortgage Last 12 Months	Consumer Last 12 Months	Bankruptcy NOD/Foreclosure	Charge offs/Judgments
_____ X 30	_____ X 30	Chapter _____	# Filed _____
_____ X 60	_____ X 60	Discharge Date:	$ Amount _____
_____ X 90	_____ X 90	_____	$ to remain open _____
_____ X 120	_____ X 120	Balances: _____	$ to be paid _____

_____ Credit Score

Credit History (12 months)
Secondary Homeowner

Mortgage Last 12 Months	Consumer Last 12 Months	Bankruptcy NOD/Foreclosure	Charge offs/Judgments
_____ X 30	_____ X 30	Chapter _____	# Filed _____
_____ X 60	_____ X 60	Discharge Date:	$ Amount _____
_____ X 90	_____ X 90	_____	$ to remain open _____
_____ X 120	_____ X 120	Balances: _____	$ to be paid _____

_____ Credit Score

CREDIT REPORT AUTHORIZATION AND RELEASE

Authorization is hereby granted to _____ to obtain a standard factual data credit report through a credit-reporting agency chosen by the _____

My signature below authorizes the release to the credit-reporting agency a copy of my credit application, and authorizes the credit-reporting agency to obtain information regarding my employment, savings accounts, and outstanding credit accounts (mortgages, auto loans, personal loans, charge cards, credit unions, etc.) Authorization is further granted to the reporting agency to use a Photostatted reproduction of this authorization if necessary to obtain any information regarding the above-mentioned information.

Applicants hereby request a copy of the credit report with any possible derogatory information be sent to the address of present residence, and holds _____ and any credit reporting organization harmless in so mailing the copy requested.

Any reproduction of this credit authorization and release made by reliable means (for example, photocopy, or facsimile is considered an original.

_____
Homeowner's Signature
Date:
SSN:

_____
Homeowner's Signature
Date:
SSN:

_____
Homeowner's Signature
Date:
SSN:

_____
Homeowner's Signature
Date:
SSN:

Figure7:9 Credit Report Authorization and Release – HUD Release

OCCUPANCY DECLARATIONS

Lender:
RE: Loan No:
        PROPERTY ADDRESS:

The undersigned Borrower of the above described property does hereby declare, under penalty of perjury, as follows:

1.   Borrower shall occupy, establish, and use the Property as Borrowers principal residence within sixty days after execution of the Security Instrument and shall continue to occupy the property as Borrower's principal residence for at least one year after the date of occupancy unless Lender otherwise agrees in writing, which consent shall not be unreasonably withheld, or unless extenuating circumstances exist which are beyond the Borrower's control.

        You are hereby informed that Lender from time to time makes spot checks for owner occupancy on properties upon which we have secured a mortgage.

        Between the first and thirteenth day, after close of escrow, occupancy may be checked more than once. If after this check Lender is to believe that you never intended to occupy the subject as your primary residence, we may choose to call your note due and payable or increase your note rate by 100 basis points, in accordance with the applicable sections itemized on your note and Security Instrument and allowable by law.

2.   Borrower shall be in default, if during the loan application process, gave materially false or inaccurate information or statements to Lender (or failed to provide Lender with material information) in connection with the loan evidenced by the Note, including, but not limited to, representations concerning Borrower's occupancy of the Property as a Principal residence.

3.   The Lender has the right to foreclose on the loan under the terms of the Security Instrument if items 1 or 2 above are violated.

4.   Should Borrower's intention change prior to close of transaction, then it is agreed that the Lender will be immediately notified of that fact.

5.   Borrower understands that without this declaration of intention, Lender may not make the loan in connection with the property.

I DECLARE, UNDER PENALTY OF PERJURY, THAT THE FOREGOING DECLARATION IS TRUE AND CORRECT.

Figure7:10 - Sample Form – Occupancy Declaration – HUD Release

UNIFORM RESIDENTIAL APPRAISAL REPORT

The purpose of this summary appraisal report is to provide with an accurate, and adequately supported opinion of market value of the subject property

Property Address		City	State	Zip Code
Borrower	Owner of Public Record		County	

Legal Description

Assessor's Parcel #		Tax Year	R.E. Taxes $
Neighborhood Name		Map Reference	Census Tract

Occupant __ Owner __ Tenant __ Vacant   Special Assessments $ _____   PUD HOA $ _____ per year _____ per month

Property Rights Appraised __ Fee Simple __ Leasehold __ Other (describe)

Assignment Type __ Purchase Transaction __ Refinance Transaction __ Other (describe)

Lender Client _____ Address

Is the subject property currently offered for sale or has it been offered for sale in the twelve months prior to the effective date of this appraisal __ yes __ no

Report data source(s) used offering prices(s), and date(s)

I __ did __ did not analyze the contract for sale for the subject purchase transaction. Explain the results of the analysis of the contract for sale or why analysis was not performed.

Contract Price $ _____ Date of Contract _____ Is the property seller the owner of public record __ Yes __ No Data Source(s)

Is there any financial assistance (loan charges, sale concessions, gift or down payment assistance, etc.) to be paid by any party on behalf of the borrower? __ Yes __ No If yes, report the total dollar amount and describe the items to be paid.

Note: Race and racial composition of the neighborhood are not appraisal factors

Neighborhood Characteristics			One-Unit Housing Trends				One-Unit Housing		Present Land Use %		
Location	Urban	Suburban	Rural	Property Values	Increasing	Stable	Declining	PRICE	AGE	One-Unit	%
Built-Up	Over 75%	25-75%	Under 25%	Demand Supply	Shortage	In Balance	Over Supply	$ (000)	(yrs)	2-4 Unit	%
Growth	Rapid	Stable	Slow	Marketing Time	Under 2 mth	3-6 mths	Over 6 mths	Low		Multi-Family	%
Neighborhood Boundaries								High		Commercial	%
								Pred.		Other	%

Neighborhood Description

Market Conditions (including support for the above conclusions)

Dimension	Area	Shape	View

Specific Zoning Classification _____ Zoning Description

Zoning Compliance __ Legal __ Legal Nonconforming (Grandfathered use) __ No Zoning __ Illegal (describe)

Is the highest and best use of the subject property as improved (or as proposed per plans and specifications) the present use? __ Yes __ No If No, describe

Utilities   Public Other (describe)   Public Other (describe)   Off-site Improvements – Type   Public
Private

Electricity	__ __	Water	__ __	Street	__
Gas	__ __	Sanitary Sewer	__ __	Alley	__

FEMA Special Hazard Area __ Yes __ No FEMAL Flood Zone _____ Fema Map # _____ FEMA Map Date

Are the utilities and off-site improvements typical for the market area __ Yes __ No If No, describe

Are there any adverse site conditions or extreme factors (easements, encroachments, environmental conditions and uses, etc.)? __ Yes __ No If Yes, describe

General Description	Foundation	Exterior Description materials/condition	Interior materials/condition
Units __ One __ One w Accessory Unit	__ Concrete Slab __ Crawl Space	Foundation Walls	Floors
# of Stories	__ Full Basement __ Partial Basement	Exterior Walls	Walls
Type __ Det __ Att __ S-Dec / End Unit	Basement Area _____ sq ft	Roof Surface	Trim/Finish
__ Existing __ Proposed __ Under Cons	Basement Finish _____ %	Gutters & Downspouts	Bath Floor
Design (Style)	__ Outside Entry/ Exist __ Sump Pump	Window Type	Bath Wainscot
Year Built	Evidence of __ Infestation	Storm Sash / Insulated	Car Storage __ None
Effective Age (Yrs)	__ Dampness __ Settlement	Screens	__ Driveway # of Cars
Attic __ None	Heating __ FWA __ HWBB __ Radiant	Amenities __ Woodstove(s)	Driveway Surface
__ Drop Stair __ Stairs	__ Other __ Fuel	__ Fireplaces # __ Fence	__ Garage # of Cars
__ Floor __ Scuttle	Cooling __ Central Air Conditioning	__ Patio/Deck __ Porch	__ Carport # of Cars
__ Finished __ Heated	__ Individual __ Other	__ Pool __ Other	__ Att __ Det __ Built-in

Appliances __ Refrigerator __ Range/Oven __ Dishwasher __ Disposal __ Microwave __ Washer/Dryer __ Other (describe)

Finished area above grade contains: _____ Rooms _____ Bedrooms _____ Bath(s) _____ Square Feet of Gross Living Area Above Grade

Additional Features (special energy efficient items, etc.)

Describe the conditions of the property (including needed repairs, deterioration, renovations, remodeling, etc.)

Are there any physical deficiencies or adverse conditions that affect the livability, soundness, or structural integrity of the property? __ Yes __ No If Yes, describe

Figure 8:1 - Sample Form – URAR – HUD Release

UNIFORM RESIDENTIAL APPRAISAL REPORT

There are	comparable properties currently offered for sale in the subject neighborhood ranging in price from $		to $	
There are	comparable sales in the subject neighborhood within the past twelve months ranging in sales price from $		to $	

FEATURE	SUBJECT	COMPARABLE SALE #1	COMPARABLE SALE #2	COMPARABLE SALE #3
Address				
Proximity to Subject				
Sale Price	$	$	$	$
Sale Price/Gross Liv Area	$ sq ft	$ sq ft	$ sq ft	$ sq ft
Data Source(s)				
Verification Source(s)				

VALUE ADJUSTMENTS	DESCRIPTION	DESCRIPTION	Adjustment	DESCRIPTION	Adjustment	DESCRIPTION	Adjustment
Sales or Financing Concessions							
Date of Sale / Time							
Location							
Leasehold/Fee Simple							
Site							
View							
Design (Style)							
Quality of Construction							
Actual Age							
Condition							
Above Grade Room Count	Total Bdrms Baths	Total Bedrms Baths		Total Brms Baths		Total Brms Baths	
Gross Living Area	sq ft	sq ft		sq ft		sq ft	
Basement & Finished Rooms Below Grade							
Functional Utility							
Heating / Cooling							
Energy Efficient							
Garage / Carport							
Porch/Patio/Deck							
Net Adjustment		+ -	$	+ -	$	+ -	$
Adjusted Sales Price of Comps		Net Adj % Gross Adj %	$	Net Adj % Gross Adj %	$	Net Adj % Gross Adj %	$

I __ did __ did not research the sale or transfer history of the subject property and comparable sales. If not, explain

My research __ did __ did not reveal any prior sales or transfers of the subject property for the three years prior to the effective date of this appraisal.
Data source(s)

My research __ did __ did not reveal any prior sales or transfers of the comparables sales for the year prior to the date of sale of the comparable sale.
Data source(s)

Report the results of the research and analysis of the prior sale or transfer history of the subject property and comparable sales (report additional on pg 3)

ITEM	SUBJECT	COMPARABLE SALE #1	COMPARABLE SALE #2	COMPARABLE SALE #3
Date of Prior Sale/Transfer				
Price of Prior Sale/Transfer				
Data Source(s)				
Effective Date of Data Source(s)				

Analysis of prior sale or transfer history of the subject property and comparable sales

Summary of Sales Comparison Approach

Indicated Value by Sales Comparison Approach $

Indicated Value by: Sales Comparison Approach $ Cost Approach (if developed) $ Income Approach (if developed) $

The appraisal is made __ as is __ subject to completion per plans and specifications on the basis of a hypothetical condition that the improvements have been completed. __ subject to the following repairs or alterations on the basis of a hypothetical condition that repairs have been completed, or __ subject to the following required inspection based on the extraordinary assumption that the condition or deficiency does not require alteration or repair.

Figure 8:7 - Sample Form – URAR – HUD Release

www.ingramcontent.com/pod-product-compliance
Lightning Source LLC
Chambersburg PA
CBHW080720220326
41520CB00056B/7218